The future has always held a fascination for mankind, but today this interest is approaching an obsession: astrology, necromancy, spiritism, witchcraft. With the growing frustrations and uncertainties of life, men are turning more and more to the future in search of ultimate reality.

We commend this volume of lectures by Dr. Wilbur M. Smith as a lucid and logical discussion of what the future holds for mankind according to the Word of God. Dr. Smith, a distinguished Bible scholar and author has devoted his life to the study and interpretation of the Scriptures and what is revealed about the future.

This book as a practical handbook on eschatology (the doctrine of final things) will provide Biblical answers to many of the searching questions people are asking. Dr. Wilbur M. Smith is currently developing a comprehensive volume on the subject for those who wish to study it in depth. This will be a most significant achievement for this author of 38 volumes of Peloubet's Notes, 21 other books on the Bible and theology, innumerable articles.

YOU CAN KNOW THE FUTURE!

Cyrus N Nelson

President, G/L Publications

YOU CAN KNOW THE FUTURE

YOU CAN KNOW THE FUTURE
WILBUR M. SMITH

A division of G/L Publications
Glendale, California, U.S.A.

© Copyright 1971 by G/L Publications
All rights reserved
Printed in U.S.A.

Published by
Regal Books Division, G/L Publications
Glendale, California, 91209, U.S.A.

Library of Congress Catalog Card No. 75-169845
ISBN 0-8307-0110-9

Contents

1. The Fascinating Future **1**
2. The Bible—A Book of Prophecy **11**
3. The Course of This Age **21**
4. The Future of Israel **31**
5. The Antichrist, Master of Deception **41**
6. He's Coming Again! **51**
7. Armageddon **61**
8. The Resurrection **71**
9. The Signs of the Times **79**
10. Final Destiny **89**
11. The Millennium **97**
12. Heaven, Our Eternal Home **109**

CHAPTER 1

The Fascinating Future

By "Biblical Eschatology," we mean the doctrine of the last things—the doctrine of the things that are yet to come—what the Bible has to say about the future.

In this introductory chapter we will refer to man's longing to know something about the future, and some ways that he has developed (though inadequately) for attempting to discover the future.

Man, by his very nature, when in a rational mood and giving serious attention to life's great problems, cannot help but ask himself and ask others what the future holds for himself, for his family, for his nation, and for this chaotic world in which he is living today. Parents must plan for an immediate future for their children. They must determine where their children will go to school, what they will wear, where they are going to live, and so on.

So, a young man graduating from college must, sooner or later, decide what he wants to do and to be in the years that are ahead of him. Most of the decisions of our vast national government have to do with the future of the United States. And, because of the great uncertainty and the peril of our particular generation, men are more fervently than ever seeking to know something of what is ahead of us. Books on this subject are multiplying with enormous rapidity. No one can even keep up with the literature that is now being published by outstanding scholars about what the future may hold. As I write, I have several of these in my hand. One, published by Little, Brown and edited by Wolfstein Holmes, is titled *Man and His Future*; one by Dr. Arthur Clark, published by Harper & Row, *Profiles of the Future*; a shorter book by Still, *Man, the Next Thirty Years*. Then there is a book that has had a tremendous sale by Kahn and Weiner, published by MacMillan, entitled *The Year 2000*, and a new book published by Indiana University, edited by Boyko, *Science and the Future of Mankind*.

So, discussing this matter of Biblical Eschatology, we find ourselves in a period when men are asking what the future holds, probably more eagerly than ever before. This goes all the way back to earliest Bible times when men are found seeking to know something about the future in a secular way. Thus, we find in Deuteronomy, the 18th chapter, verses 9, 10 and 11, a very interesting passage: *Thou shalt not learn to do after the abominations of those nations,* that is, the pagan nations around Israel. Now Moses becomes specific here: *There shall not be found among you any one who maketh his son or his daughter to pass through the fire, or that useth divination, or an observer of times, or an enchanter, or a witch, or a charmer, or a consulter with familiar spirits, or a wizard, or a necromancer.*

Here are eight different ways in which these pagan nations attempted to find out something about the future. These are secular means, and the mosaic law here says that Israel is not to dabble in this.

Notice this word, *divination*. This is the general term for efforts to discern the future in Greek and Latin culture. You remember that Cicero wrote a book on divination, *De Divinatione*, at the end of which he condemned the whole process of divination.

Recently, something dawned on me. This is a very simple matter but it took me years to see it. If you take these opening letters, d-i-v-i-n and put an "e" on the end of them, you've got divine. Thus, when one is practicing divination, he is almost attempting to reach God or to discover the plan of the gods. He may think that what he is doing is divine in itself, which of course is wickedness.

Now, inasmuch as man normally is at times truly concerned about the future, he has developed all these different ways in which he can quiet his heart and know something about the days ahead. To ask about the future is not wrong, but we are to turn to the record that God has given us for an answer to our problem. You remember that day on Tuesday of Holy Week when the disciple said to Jesus, *What is the sign of Thy coming and when will these things take place?* And then you remember at the opening of the Book of Acts, where the disciples asked Jesus: *Wilt thou at this time restore the kingdom to Israel?* Over and over again in the Old Testament you have the psalmists and the prophets crying out, *How long, Oh Lord, how long?*

Now let us look at some of the means that were used in the ancient world for attempting to discover the future. Our purpose is to indicate some of the ways in which the ancient world, and even the modern world (the ancient world without the Word of God—the modern world in many cases spurning the Word of God), attempted and attempt to look into the future.

Under this word divination, which includes direct divination, indirect divination and dreams, divination took many, many forms. I want to examine this because it was tremendously important in those days. There was a science known as hepatoscopy. This refers to the examination of the livers of slain sheep in an effort to discern what one should do, go to war, or not go to war, or who was to be the next king, and so on and so on. This was practiced as long ago as two thousand and eight hundred years before Christ.

Now, don't think this was something obscure or secondary. Actually, there were hundreds of priests in Babylon and Assyria whose entire lifetime was devoted to the interpretation of what they found in the livers of sheep. They marked up these livers in certain squares, and, if there was a swelling in one place or decayed matter in another place, or if the liver was perfectly rounded, and so on, all these different forms and contents took on various symbolic meanings. Remember this was the official method in the vast empires of Babylonia, and Assyria for attempting to discern the future.

Other devices used were the flight of birds, certain formations of water, and so on. All these pagan ideas, of course, are now dispensed with.

Then, there is the agelong practice of astrology beginning hundreds of years before our Lord and, of course, practiced today. We have scores of magazines on our shelves, in drug stores and magazine stores, devoted entirely to the determination of one's future by the location of the stars in the zodiac, at the time of one's birth.

I remember sitting in an airplane some three or four years ago, next to a man who was on his way to Chicago to deliver a scientific message. He was the head of the promotion department of one of the greatest chemical firms in America. He was a man about forty-five or fifty years of age, who of course must have had ability or he wouldn't have had this position. I suppose he earned forty or fifty thousand dollars a year. We got to talking about the Lord and about the Bible, and he reached into his breast pocket and took out a little square piece of thin wood on which were marked the locations of certain stars. He said, "This is my future, this is my fortune. If I will just follow the direction of what these stars indicate, week by week, month by month, and year by year, according to the rotation of certain stars in the heavens and the planets when I was born, then I will never do anything wrong and will be successful." So, I said to him, "What do you do for praying? You don't pray to the planets, do you?" "No," he said, "but I don't need to pray; I have the guidance of the stars." This is astrology. Man attempting to discover the future from the location of the planets and of the movement of the stars in the heavens.

Then, there was what we call the consultation of oracles. The Greeks had a great many of these, while Rome didn't care much for them. Men began to be too wise for this about the time the Roman Empire was established. But the Greeks continually consulted oracles, especially in Delphi, a gorgeously beautiful place in Northern Greece. There they would find a strange appearing woman sitting on a tripod in a deep cavern or crevice in the rock. These messengers to the oracles asked certain questions of attending priests. "Shall we go to war with Persia? Will Persia win this conflict? Shall we cross such and such a river? Shall we join with Sparta? Shall so and so get married?" There was always a priest nearby. The woman would utter strange words as fumes arose around her. Then, the priest would interpret what this woman was saying to the messenger who had come from some far-away king or royal court. Don't think this was a minor thing in Greece. They built some of the most gorgeous temples in the world at the sites of these oracles, and each temple had a rich treasury. At one time when Delphi was at its heights, millions and millions of dollars of precious jewels and monies of all kinds were accumulated in the treasuries of these temples which can now be seen in ruin at Delphi and other ancient cities.

There is another way of attempting to know the future. We might call it that of historical structure. This pretends to tell us the way history is going to go. You may not be so sure about your own future, your family and maybe your neighborhood or nation, but this is the way history is going to go. There have been many, many books on this. One view is what is called "The Morphological View." This was developed by Spengler, the great German historian, who died a few years ago. It was his theory that the human race or Western Civilization is like a plant: the plant has to have an origin, that is, it has to have an initial stage. And then it has to grow vigorously; and finally it produces fruit. After it has grown to its full height and has produced the fruit that was expected of it, then it begins to wilt. Ultimately it loses its strength and vitality and withers away. Now said Spengler, this is what is going to happen to European civilization. It had its root in the Greek and Roman cultures; it grew slowly in the Middle Ages; then it burst out in the Renaissance, the Reformation and the subsequent centuries, the 17th, 18th, 19th and 20th. Spengler insisted European civilization is now declining. The Oriental nations will now come forth, and they will be strong and vigorous. Europe may well expect to go into a decline and finally be overwhelmed in its own weakness. So far, it hasn't turned out that way. Germany was beaten in two shocking wars, but Germany, especially West Germany, is vigorous today, and the rest of Europe also is showing great vigor. So Spengler's theory has not been justified by the course of events in Europe in the last thirty or forty years.

Then there was a theory which was very prominent after Darwin's Origin of the Species in 1859. Beginning about 1870 and to about 1915, there was a great rash of books and thousands of articles on what is called "Inevitable Progress," affirming that mankind is going from one great invention to another, from one great development in science to another—prosperity abounding and increasing on every hand. Famines and other major problems would be eliminated. This was called the theory of inevitable historical progress. Now this was all right until the first World War, and then of course progress became regress. Millions of people were killed, and the bitterness and the ugliness and the inhumanity of the human heart were revealed. Then we had Woodrow Wilson with the hope of the world and the League of Nations and—still more inevitable progress. Then came the Second World War, when millions more were killed, and six million Jews were destroyed in Germany and Central Europe, and Germany became guilty of crimes that appalled the world. Of Communism in Russia it has been written, "Since the rise of Communism in Russia, 25 million people in Russia have been exterminated." So this theory of inevitable progress is disproved. We now read of professors giving lectures, as one did recently in a famous college in New England in which he said, "We are at the edge of the abyss; we are in ultimate universal peril; we are on the verge of destroying ourselves." I am only quoting. So this whole philosophy of inevitable progress has disintegrated under the terrible pressure of the reality of contemporary facts.

Then there is Marxism. The strange thing about Marxism and Communism is that while they have a lot to do with the future, it is not so much with the future of contemporary man. I don't think it's selfish to say that you and I are interested in our own future as well as in the future of our nation. A Communist wouldn't say that. He is interested in world Communism that may not even come in his own time. He has a future— a future for the next generation and maybe the next century. And he has developed a philosophical system by which all mankind will be leveled. There will be no unemployment, no hunger, and prosperity will be equally allotted to all. We have seen enough of Marxism and Communism that we need not be envious.

Then there is what we might call the future imagined by the poets. It is the dreaming of a great and glorious day of paradise yet ahead. Tennyson did this in his poem "Locksley Hall," 1842—a hundred and thirty years ago when the world thought it was really a paradise. Let me quote some of it to you. "Men, my brothers, men the workers, ever reaping something new, That which they have done but earnest of the things that they shall do, For I dipped into the future, far as human eye could see, Saw the vision of the world and all the wonder that would be. Till the war drum throbs no longer and the battle flags were furled, In the parliament of man the federation of the world."

World peace, so Tennyson thought, was imminent: "In the parliament of man the federation of the world." He was looking into the future, but he saw it in error. He saw it optimistically, when really it was to be a pessimistic future. Even he knew this, for toward the end of his life, in 1886, he wrote another poem called "Locksley Hall, Sixty Years After." And here are two lines "sixty years after": "I myself, have often dabbled doubtless of a foolish past. Dabbled, dabbled, our old

England may go down in battle at last." And so it did in the two world wars.

Now so much for the poets' attempt to discover the future. Years ago when I was in my late teens attending a great world Christian Endeavor Convention in the Coliseum in Chicago, a huge banner was unfurled across the great front of that auditorium which proclaimed "A Warless World by 1920." It was a good dream—a great goal, but that isn't the way it turned out.

The human heart, naturally, inevitably longs to know something about the future. The more uncertain, the greater the dreadful possibilities of the day in which we live, the more man seems to be eager to discover some basic things he can depend upon in the future. This is natural, this is inevitable for man.

Man has attempted in many, many different ways down through the ages to discover something definite about the future—generally the immediate future. In the whole world, of the millions of books at Harvard, at the Library of Congress, at the British Museum, in Chicago and elsewhere in all languages—there is only one divine book that contains a divine revelation, the Bible. This is the revelation from heaven concerning the things that are to take place on this earth—your future, my future, the future of the nations of the earth, the future of Israel, the future of the world and the future of mankind. This is all unveiled to us in the goodness and mercy of God. So as this Word of God enters into our hearts, it becomes a lamp unto our feet and a light unto our pathway. It delivers us from the deceptions of false and materialistic and humanistic attempts to discover the future. In these holy pages we have the Word of Truth—truth about the past, the present and the future.

CHAPTER 2

The Bible—A Book of Prophecy

As we begin our second discussion of eschatology, perhaps we ought to look at the word eschatology for just a moment. It comes directly out of the Greek language. In the New Testament we have the word *eschaton* from which we derive this word "eschatology." It means principally "the last," as in Matthew 20:16, *The last shall be first*. But it generally refers to *the last days*, to the end of this age, as in John the sixth chapter beginning with verse 39, our Lord said of the dead, (He) *would raise it up again at the last day*. In Acts 2:17, you have the phrase *The last days*. The Apostle Paul begins his third chapter of II Timothy with the phrase, *In the last days*. So eschatology is really the doctrine of the last things.

The Bible is a book of prediction, of prophetic utterances. This is illustrated by its very vocabulary. When we speak of the *prophecies* of the Bible, we should keep in mind, first, that many prophecies were long ago fulfilled as Isaiah 53, the birth of Jesus in Bethlehem; Micah 5:2, etc. The things which God had shown by the mouth of all the prophets that Christ should suffer, *he hath so fulfilled* (Acts 3:18). Thus many of the prophecies in the Bible have already occurred. Some prophecies are in the *process* of being fulfilled, as Matthew 13:24-30, the parable of the wheat and the tares and in Matthew 24:5-14, the description of the course of this age. Some have been fulfilled, some are being fulfilled, but a great number of prophecies both in the Old Testament and the New are *yet* to be fulfilled, as Isaiah 11, the great battle of Ezekiel 38 and 39, the tribulation of Matthew 24:29-31, the coming of Antichrist, the second advent of our Lord, and many others.

So let us now look at what we might call prophetic nomenclature—that is, words used in the Bible to indicate matters pertaining to the future.

First, the words "prophet," "prophecy" and "prophesy." The noun "prophet" occurs 315 times in the Old Testament and 156 times in the New Testament! The verbal form "prophesy" occurs 110 times in the Old Testament and 28 times in the New. These prophecies we call "prophecy" a word which occurs 22 times in the Old and New Testaments. Here you have three words, "prophet," "prophesy," and "prophecy" occurring 641 times in the Old and New Testaments. Some men who were really called prophets did not actually utter predictions of far off events but foretold God's message, as Elijah in First Kings 17:24. Some prophets had a wider ministry than that of foretelling, as Elisha. But normally a prophet was one who foretold the future.

A second important word is the word "promise," which we too often neglect. A truly wonderful word! The word "promise" is frequently used in the Bible in relation to the prediction of events yet to take place, as in Acts 13:23, *God, according to his promise.* This is a reference, of course, to that great series of prophecies in Genesis 12, 13, 15, 22, 26 and 35 when God promised to Abraham, and to Isaac and Jacob, that they would have a great seed, and they would possess the land of Palestine. In fact, Palestine is actually referred to as *The land of promise,* and you may be surprised where this is. You would think that it is an Old Testament designation, but this phrase *the land of promise* is only in Hebrews 11:9.

Some of these promises are for all of us. Jews and Gentiles who are in Christ as in II Peter 3:13, *According to His promise,* (we) *look for new heavens and a new earth, wherein dwelleth righteousness.* This word "righteousness" is tremendously important in relation to what God is ultimately going to do on this earth. When Paul was addressing the Athenian philosophers, he said that when Christ came *He would judge the world in righteousness.* I think sometimes we forget, with this great sweeping criminal wave of unrighteousness and dishonesty, that righteousness is the one thing that is going to be stamped upon the civilization which our Lord Himself will establish in that millennial reign.

Now we have looked at two words, prophet and promise. The third is, "the end." This is a term of particular prophetic nature, especially in the Book of Daniel where you have references to the time of the end in 8:17, 19, chapter 11:27, 35 and others. Our Lord Himself in the great Olivet Discourse refers to *The end* (Matthew 24:14). Related to these references is I Corinthians 15:24.

"The end," is a closely related title to, "the times" or "the last days." This is referred to significantly for the first time at the end of the Book of Genesis in that great 49th chapter where the futures of the twelve sons of Jacob are unfolded. There we find the phrase, *the last days* (Genesis 49:1). We have it in Joel 2:28-31 which Saint Peter quoted on the day of Pentecost in Acts, chapter 2.

"The last day" is a phrase often used by our Lord, as in John 6:39,40. The Apostle Paul used it in addressing Timothy in his second Epistle 3:1. We find it also in I Peter, the first chapter and the fifth verse.

Other terms relating to the predicting of future events are such words as *foretell*, Mark 13:23 and II Peter 3:2, or *to testify before hand*, I Peter 1:11. A great statement relating to the subject we are discussing is that of St. Paul in the address I referred to a moment ago to the Athenian philosophers. Notice this phrase, (God) *hath determined the times before appointed* (Acts 17:26). This is most comforting! Not Hitler, not Communism, not Antichrist, but it is God who *hath determined the times appointed.*

Also, an interesting phrase is in Galatians 3:8, *The Scripture, foreseeing*. There are four words, all beginning with the letter *R*, in fact, all beginning with the little syllable *re*. Four words of profound meaning connected with these future times. These are, "Restitution," as in the *times of restitution*, Acts 3:21. *Times of refreshing*, Acts 3:19. *The reformation*, Hebrews 9:10. And *the time of the regeneration*, Matthew 19:28. This little syllable *re*, these two letters, always mean "again," the second time—the restitution, refreshing, restoration, regeneration. This is what God will bring about.

Now there are two prerequisites if God's predictions are to come true—two things about God that must be true if His Word will ultimately be fulfilled. God must know all things that are yet to come, which is one aspect of His omniscience. If God did not foreknow all that would occur in the future, it might be that forces unknown to God would appear to thwart His purposes and prevent some prophecy or some series of prophecies being fulfilled. Let me quote a helpful word from the distinguished theologian, Dr. Berkhoff, in his *Systematic Theology*.

"The free knowledge of God is the knowledge which he has of all things active. That is of things that existed in the past, that exist in the present or that will exist in the future. It is founded on God's infinite knowledge of his own all-comprehensive and unchangeable eternal purpose. He knows the hidden essence of things to which the knowledge of man cannot penetrate." Psalms 33:13 and 139:2,4.

Not only must God be *omniscient,* but He must be able to bring to pass whatsoever He has foreordained. He must be *omnipotent.* Now you and I can talk about the future, our own; what we are going to do for our children, and what they are going to do. But we are not omnipotent. We have plans, but we may not have the strength to bring them to pass. We may even die before they are fulfilled. But God is all powerful. If He were not, who knows but that Satan and his powerful hosts could prevent the fulfilling of many of these prophecies. May I remind you here, and interject something from the Book of Revelation which we will look at sometime later—such words as army, might, power, king, rule, authority, dominion. Have you ever noticed that all of these words are not only used in relation to Christ but are also used in relation to Satan and Antichrist. All have power, all have an army, all have a throne. But there is one word in the Book of Revelation which, thank God, is never used in reference to any evil power at all. This is the word, *Almighty* (Revelation 1:8). Thus, because God is all powerful, we are assured that He is able to bring to pass whatsoever He has foreordained.

Here is a great passage, Isaiah 14:24, *The Lord of*

hosts hath sworn, saying, Surely as I have thought, so shall it come to pass; and as I have purposed, so shall it stand. One should consider especially the tremendous words in Isaiah 46:8-11. *Remember this, and show yourselves men: bring it again to mind, O ye transgressors. Remember the former things of old: for I am God, and there is none else; I am God, and there is none like me, declaring the end from the beginning, and from ancient times the things that are not yet done, saying My counsel shall stand, and I will do all my pleasure: calling a ravenous bird from the east, the man that executeth my counsel from a far country: yea, I have spoken it, I will also bring it to pass; I have purposed it, I will also do it.* What wonderful words—true of no one else in the whole universe.

These prophecies of the Bible include all of mankind. No one escapes, no matter what his religion is. The prophecies of the scripture embrace the entire humanity, including a judgment to come, and the ultimate destiny of the wicked. Not only do Biblical prophecies embrace all of mankind, but they embrace all times. It is not that at a certain period the prophecies of the Bible are going to be fulfilled and then some more prophecies mentioned by someone else are going to be fulfilled. The Word of God, the Old and New Testaments, carries us down to *the last days,* to the time of resurrection, to the time of judgment, to the time of the designation of the souls of men to their eternal destiny.

Now there is something else in this matter of prophecy we should remember. It relates to the three persons of the God Head: God the Father, Christ the Son, and the Holy Spirit. There are three verses pertaining to these three themes. First God: Isaiah 46:9, 10, *I am God, and there is none like me, declaring the end from the beginning, and from ancient times the things that are not yet done.* Incidentally have you ever looked carefully into this phrase, "ancient times?" How ancient? I wouldn't be a bit surprised, and we have to be very careful here, if there were prophecies uttered by God the Father that we do not have in scripture; that He didn't intend for us to have in scripture. There may have been prophecies other than the third chapter of Genesis, between that and the time of the flood—from ancient times, so that from the very beginning, from the fall of man there was this invasion of the prophetic themes of divine purpose.

Second, our Lord is related to prophecy. Here is an interesting phrase that I have never spoken on, that I've never read anything on (Mark 13:23). It is only in Mark. *Behold I have foretold you all things.* These are words of our Lord in whom was the spirit of prophecy.

Third, prophecy is related to the Holy Spirit. In our Lord's last discourse on Thursday of Holy Week, in John 16:13 we read, *When he, the Spirit of truth, is come . . . He will show you things to come.*

So *God* declares the end from the beginning. Jesus said, *I have foretold you all things.* And the Holy Spirit is sent that He may show us things to come. Do you know what this implies? That God wants us to know something about the future—to be comforted in what He has revealed about the future and, for others, to be warned about what the future may be if they are outside of Christ.

We are at the end of this second message, and we will get into particular areas of prediction in the third chapter. I would like to just outline for you what we hope to do in this series of studies on eschatology.

There are many things that are predicted in the scriptures—recorded in the vast areas of prediction.

There are prophecies of individuals, as of Abraham, Genesis 12:1-3.

Then there are prophecies regarding cities, as Nineveh in the Book of Nahum. Of course hundreds of them concern Jerusalem, especially the last chapters of Isaiah.

First individuals, then cities, and then nations. This body of prophecy regarding nations is the most neglected area of prophetic study. Let me refer you to the great cluster of prophecies regarding nations in the Old Testament: Isaiah 13:17, Jeremiah 46-51, and Ezekiel 25-32.

Then fourth, in the book of Daniel, we have prophecies regarding the great empires, (chapters 2 and 7).

Fifth, we have the wonderful Messianic prophecies beginning in the third chapter of Genesis and going straight into the New Testament, regarding the first and second advent.

Sixth, the prophecies concerning Israel. They are innumerable.

Seventh, prophecies regarding the Church, as in Acts 20: 29, 30.

Eighth, the great prophetic discourse of our Lord concerning the course of this age in Matthew 24:25; Mark 13; and Luke 21.

Ninth, the end of the age, the great tribulation.

Tenth, the second advent of our Lord.

Eleventh, the resurrection of the just and the unjust.

Twelfth, the millennial reign of Christ.

Thirteenth, our eternal home in heaven.

Fourteenth, the last judgment.

Fifteenth, celestial disturbances, as in Joel 2:28-32.

Sixteenth and last, a new heaven and a new earth.

The only volume in all the world in which all these glorious themes are revealed to us is the Bible. These prophecies deserve a lifetime of study and an eternal study in glory too.

Of course, don't forget, that there are many, many

important subjects that are not referred to in the Holy Scriptures. I don't think there is anything in the Bible about the Reformation, although some may think so (in the seven churches of Asia). I don't think there is anything in the Book of Revelation about Napoleon Bonaparte, though I have two or three books that tell me there is. And I am sure that there is no particular prophecy about the United States, although many books have been written on this too. Our own country is included in the predictions concerning all the nations of the earth, but there is no particular reference either to the United States or, as some used to think, Japan.

If my own calculations are even approximately correct, there are about one hundred sixty-five thousand words of predictive prophecy in the Bible. This is about the equivalent of two thirds of the entire text of the New Testament. And it will come as a surprise to many, I am sure, that there is more prophetic material in Matthew, Mark and Luke than there is prophetic material in the entire Book of Revelations.

CHAPTER 3

The Course of This Age

We now come to our third in this series of studies of Biblical Eschatology. The two previous chapters were more or less preliminary—man's desire to know something about the future, and the fact that in the Bible we have truly a predictive literature. This third subject I am calling "The course of this age."

By *this age* we mean the entire period from the ascension of our Lord until His return. There are many, many prophecies in the Old and the New Testament regarding the end of the age and our Lord's return, resurrection and judgment. But this particular subject, "The course of this age," that is, what the New Testament has to say will happen from the time of the beginning of the church to the end of this age, is a subject greatly negected.

First of all we have this initial statement in the 13th chapter of Matthew regarding the simultaneous growth *of wheat and tares,* which has to do with *this age.* Notice, verses 37 to 40. *He that soweth the good seed is the Son of man; the field is the world; the good seed are the children of the kingdom; but the tares are the children of the wicked one; the enemy that sowed them is the devil; the harvest is the end of the world; and the reapers are the angels. As therefore the tares are gathered and burned in the fire; so shall it be in the end of this world.*

This is one of those famous seed parables, that embraces all the centuries since the ministry of the Son of man to the end of this age. Tares themselves are worthless while wheat is nourishing. Indeed, tares may prove poisonous to cattle. They take the space and the nutriment of the soil that the wheat should have. In their early stage they look like early wheat stalks. Now note carefully. *His enemy came.* This is Satan. The Greek word is from the same root as the word enmity in Genesis 3:15. It is not simple failure that we have here, but a deliberate attempt to counteract and so to destroy the work of God.

The leading Roman Catholic philosopher in France today, Maritain, gives large place to this parable in his *Philosophy of History.* May I quote just four lines: "One of the automatic laws" says Maritain, "is the quite general and simple law according to which wheat and tares grow together in human history."

Tares began to appear in the wheat even before the end of that first century. St. Paul warned the Ephesian elders of such an invasion of error, Acts: 20:29. The church at Colone was already being endangered with false philosophy, Colossians 2:18-23. St. Peter warned the church of false prophets—of those who had forsaken the right way, and scoffers in II Peter 2:15-22.

St. Paul made frequent references to such tragedies especially in his later epistles where he refers to teachers of error, I Timothy 1:6,7 II Timothy 2:18, and of those that depart from the faith, of the time when men would turn away from the truth. And St. John at the end of the century grieved that even then there were many antichrists who were denying that Jesus was the Christ, I John 2:18-22. This is what our Lord meant by the sowing of the tares by Satan in the wheat, and the simultaneous growth of wheat and tares in every generation and every century from His advent down to His return. This is one aspect of "the course of this age".

Now let us take a second statement from the Gospels relating to the course of this age. We should remember that when we have certain statements about the end of the age there could be a long preparation preceding the actual fact at the end. Thus, St. Paul says that at the end of the age there will be a great apostasy; but there could be preliminary movements leading up to this apostasy. Our Lord in the Olivet Discourse said there would be a riotous, anarchistic, lawless outburst which would be led up to by preliminary violence.

There is a significant question we should look at now. Luke 18:8 is the only place in the Gospels it occurs. *When the Son of man cometh, shall he find faith on the earth?* Phillips Translation reads like this: *When the son of man comes, will he find men on earth who believe in him?* I call your attention to the great work by the late Bishop J.C. Ryle of the 19th Century called *Expository Thoughts on the Gospels.* They are some of the richest volumes on the Gospels that have ever appeared in the English language. On this particular verse Bishop Ryle has a good statement. "There will be comparatively few believers upon the earth when Christ comes again. True faith will be found as rare as it was in the days of Noah, when only eight persons entered the ark. And in the days of Lot when only four persons left Sodom."

Heinrich Meyer, one of the greatest German commentators of the 19th Century, echoes this thought, "In connection with the glad promise which Jesus has just given in reference to the elect, there comes painfully into his consciousness the thought of a want of faith in him he would nevertheless meet with at the second coming. This he expresses in the sorrowful question, 'When the son of man cometh will he find faith on the earth?'"

The great Prime Minister of England and a devout believer, William E. Gladstone, when over eighty years of age, looking back over the 19th Century, wrote to a friend of his (in 1893) the following words: "I am driven back more and more upon the question, 'When the son of man cometh shall he find faith on earth?'"

We have a lot of confirmations here, though it is not our purpose to teach confirmations. Recently, a review of a book from an Evangelical paper was sent to me. In this book, the virgin birth, the miracles and the resurrection of our Lord are repudiated and relegated to the area of mythology. Now the tragedy is that this book got three or four reviews in the journals of this great denomination. And all of the journals recommended it. If this keeps on, and we have this insidiously in many areas, it doesn't mean that people won't go to church, or that we will not have beautiful buildings. It doesn't even mean we won't have men in the pulpit. It means that people will not have a sound faith in the great truths of the Gospel.

We have looked at two things already—that is the wheat and the tares in our study of "this age." There is a third group of verses in the New Testament that have reference to "this age" and that is the persecution which believers may expect—especially as the age draws to an end. This may be true with you, but I have never been persecuted for my faith in the Lord Jesus or for preaching. We must remember that while you and I are free from this persecution, millions and millions have suffered from it. In the days gone by in this century there has occurred the awful murder of millions of Christians in Russia. And who knows how many hundreds of thousands in China and thousands in Northern Korea have been put to death. Our Lord brings this up early in His ministry in Matthew, the 5th chapter, verses 10, 12 and 44 and in Luke 6:22. But especially in the Olivet Discourse in Luke 21:12 and in Matthew, the 24th chapter, and Mark 13:13. This is particularly emphasized, strange to say, not only in the Olivet Discourse, but in the Gospel which has very little prophetic material, the Gospel of John, John 15:18-25 and John 17:14.

We have looked so far at three different factors—three characteristics of the "course of this age": there will be tares among the wheat, there will be a decline of faith in the great truths relating to the Lord Jesus and there will be manifest in some areas and in some periods more intensely—this persecution of the followers of Christ.

Now we come to the fourth characteristic of "this age," which is basic and most important, the marvelous Olivet Discourse. This is by far, I would think, the most important single passage on the future in the New Testament outside of the Revelation. It is the most extensive prophecy that our Lord ever uttered. It is a very strange thing that we do not have in the English language today any great book exhaustively dealing with this tremendous discourse. Yet we have at least fifty books on the Sermon on the Mount, which has to do with ethics. In fact, in Bible dictionaries you will find long articles on the Sermon on the Mount, but I don't know any Bible dictionary in which there is an article on the Olivet Discourse.

The Olivet Discourse breaks into three successive sections. There is the period *before* the Tribulation, there is the period *during* the Tribulation, and, there is the period *after* the Tribulation.

This preliminary section, that is, what will happen between our Lord's first advent and the beginning of the Tribulation, appears in three Gospels, with warnings about deceptions, especially about false christs and false prophets. It is very significant that the Olivet Discourse opens with this warning: "Be not deceived, be not deceived." Why do you think our Lord begins that way? Because when it comes to prophecy many people can so easily be deceived. Nobody knows what is going to happen in the future except by the Word of God. Now you can't deceive people about the past. You can't say that George Washington was born in the 19th century—we know better. You can't say that Abraham Lincoln died in 1895—we know better. You *can* deceive people about things that are coming. One man can say, "I know what is coming," when really he doesn't, but many will believe him. And we have a lot of this in modern cults.

Those false prophets and false christs referred to by our Lord are here to teach and proclaim that which is contrary to the great fundamental truths of our faith. They will be especially effective at the end of the age because that will be a time when convulsions, political and probably physical, will be occurring on the earth—when men's hearts will be failing them for fear. When any clear-minded individual will be aware of the imminence of catastrophic events, and being without the Word of God and without Christ, he will be in a mood to grasp eagerly some utterance that claims to be from God.

Mohammed was the supreme false prophet of the past century. And the fact that millions believed in him and not in Christ is a token of what will happen at the end of the age when he who is called the false prophet will appear.

Let me be very careful here. A false christ is different from a false prophet. And Christ predicted both of them. A false christ does not simply preach and teach and proclaim what is contrary to the revealed Word of God, but he actually sets himself up as the Messiah. There had been many of these, especially in Israel, from the days of Bar Cochba down to the 19th Century. I have a book in my library written by a Jewish Rabbi on the 16 false messiahs. This is very, very significant. Israel never had a false messiah until she crucified her first true Messiah.

Immediately following in all the three records of the Olivet Discourse is the famous prediction about wars and rumors of wars. The words of Christ concerning the end of the age were, at the close of the 19th century and the beginning of the 20th century, almost entirely ignored, not only in commentaries on the Gospels but in articles dealing with war in relation to the New Testament. Many tried to escape the significance of our Lord's words.

For instance, a textbook entitled *Peace Study Textbook*, issued by some leading churches in our country, was written in 1913 just before the First World War. The author, referring to Mark 13:17, made this terrible statement: "The events that Christ foresaw and spoke of happened nearly 1850 years ago." Now notice, and we are quoting from a church publication, "And we have therefore no right to tie His words to the present or the future." Within a year the First World War would break out, and failure to give just consideration to our Lord's clear declaration regarding war has let the great proponents of international peace to make the most beautiful, but fantastic, predictions. They utter great phrases that appeal to a waiting humanity but do not spring from the study of the scriptures.

Today we have war confronting us on television, on radio, in our newspapers, every twenty-four hours. There is in one passage something about wars and *rumors* of wars, and I want to dwell on this. This word translated rumor is *akoe,* meaning what is heard and then what is talked about. In ordinary speech, rumor is something that may not be true. But things that are talked about are frankly discussed as though they were true. The Greek word here means "talk". When does any daily newspaper appear today without some article on war, generally on the first page? So we have not only war today, we have the constant talk about war. War in Congress, war in Parliament, war in the United Nations is being discussed.

In Luke 21:9 there is the word translated commotions meaning disorder and disturbances (also found in I Corinthians 14:33 and II Corinthians 6:5). In the Greek Old Testament this Greek word is used in reference to Cain as a wanderer. In Luke 21:9,11 the word *phobeetron* is translated "terror". In Matthew 24:12 is a most significant phrase, especially for a day such as ours: *Iniquity shall abound,* the word *anomia,* meaning lawlessness. This is exactly the word used in II Thessalonians 2:8, when the Apostle Paul says: *The day will come when the lawless one will appear.* And we are preparing for His advent in the lawlessness of this present age such as the world has never seen before.

There is one more statement. We are talking now about the course of this age—what Jesus said would take place between the first advent and the end of the age before the tribulation. There is one statement and only one in this entire section that predicts a victory for the Gospel. It is in Matthew 24:14 and Mark 13:10. This is the only bright, hopeful, encouraging word in this part of the Olivet Discourse. I read: *This gospel of the kingdom shall be preached in all the world for a witness unto all nations; and then shall the end come.*

What does all this mean? That all these forces antagonistic to the Christian way will not be able to suppress the furtherance of the Gospel. "All nations" appears in Matthew 28:19 and Luke 24:47. It does not imply that the whole world will be saved, but it clearly predicts that the whole world will be hearing the Gospel. What great agency, since the beginning of the 20th century, has been launched in the world—in this unbelieving, materialistic, anarchistic world—for the fulfilling of this very prediction of our Lord? It is radio! Religious paid broadcasting, or religious broadcasting over commercial stations began in Pittsburgh just 50 years ago. And now we have 300,000 hours a year devoted to the proclamation of the Gospel on radios around the world. Then there are television messages, especially those in Billy Graham's wonderful Crusades. There are Gospel recordings, Campus Crusade, and the marvelous work of Wycliffe Bible Translators. This is exactly what the Lord said. *This Gospel shall be preached in all the world for a witness unto all nations; and then shall the end come.*

CHAPTER 4

The Future of Israel

The Future of Israel is one of the most comprehensive, inexhaustible themes in the Word of God.

As we examined "The Course of This Age", we could consider only New Testament passages because they are the only ones that have reference specifically to the period between the two advents of our Lord. But, "The Future of Israel" embraces both the Old Testament and the New Testament. And we should remember, as we begin, that there are many prophecies concerning Israel in the Old Testament that have already been fulfilled—many of them. There is one great prophecy in the New Testament concerning Israel which has already been fulfilled. That is the destruction of the city of Jerusalem in A.D. 70 (Luke 21:20-24).

There are four factors regarding Israel's present condition which must be considered. First, for centuries, and in spite of the State of Israel, the Jews are scattered upon the face of the earth as the Bible said they would be in Deuteronomy 4:27,28; 28:63-67; Amos 9:1-10; etc.

Second, an amazing prediction is in Hosea 3:4, one of the great statements of the Old Testament: *For the children of Israel shall abide many days without king, and without a prince, and without a sacrifice, and without an image, and without an ephod and without teraphim.* This implies that Israel for a long time was to be without a king, without a priest, and without a prophet. And it should be recognized that Israel has had no king since Zedekiah, (598-587 B.C.); and has had no priest since the destruction of Jerusalem in A.D. 70. And the Jews admit that the last true prophet they had was John the Baptist.

Third, Israel is in a state of blindness, as stated in Romans 11:7-10, but especially in II Corinthians 3:13-16. *Not as Moses, which put a veil over his face, that the children of Israel could not steadfastly look to the end of that which is abolished: but their minds were blinded; for until this day remaineth the same veil untaken away in the reading of the old testament; which veil is done away in Christ. But even unto this day, when Moses is read, the veil is upon their heart.*

Fourth, Israel will know the perpetual hatred of the Edomites, that is the Arabs, as in Ezekiel 35:5 and especially in Psalm 83. The great Hebrew scholar of a former generation, Pusey, is correct in his statement, made about 1870, "What Edom had done and what had befallen Judah were types of the future development of the fate of Judah. And the attitudes of Edom towards it will go on fulfilling themselves more and more until the day of the Lord shall come to all nations."

These are some basic factors regarding Israel's present condition.

Our second major consideration is, the relation of Israel to the land of promise, i.e. the Holy Land. This is one of the most acute problems in the international situation, debated before the United Nations, argued continually in books—pro and con—the relation of Israel to Palestine.

This land of Palestine was promised to Israel for a perpetual possession. It begins with Genesis 12:1,7 and especially 13:14,15, Jeremiah 16:15 (many other passages in Jeremiah), Amos 9:14,15, Ezekial 37, etc. I never tire of quoting a marvelous statement on this subject of the Jews and Palestine which was written by a famous German theologian of a century ago, J. H. Kurtz. These are only four lines, but they should almost be memorized. "As the body is adapted and destined for the soul, and the soul for the body so is Israel adapted for that country and that country for Israel. Without Israel the land is like a body from which the soul has fled. Banished from its country, Israel is like a ghost which cannot find rest." I am going to repeat that last sentence again: "Without Israel the land is like a body from which the soul has fled."

I first went to Palestine in 1926. There were very few Jews in the land then. It was almost totally an Arab country, Christian Arabs as well as Mohammedan Arabs. Everything was quiet and peaceful and, one might say, restful. I saw millions of acres of desert or abandoned hillsites that today are covered with grape vines and citrus trees by the millions. Now this great change never happened until Israel came in. The land was like a ghost. It was basically uncultivated and thus without prosperity. I repeat this sentence: "Without Israel"—and *my* what she has done to that land today —"the land is like a body from which the soul has fled.

Banished from its country, Israel is like a ghost that cannot find rest."

One of the great Oriental scholars of our day, Dr. Cyrus Gordon, not, I think, a Christian believer, but an Orthodox Jew, on this matter has expressed the view of the Jews throughout the ages in these words: "These are great words that make history, the words we have in Genesis and the words we have in Deuteronomy. Centuries later in the time of Ezra and Nehemiah people thought that these words were being fulfilled, but history has shown that the second commonwealth was not the fulfillment of Amos' prophecy. But Amos' immortal words will continue to cry out for fulfillment until every promise comes true . . . His words are inseparable from the vigor of Israel down to the present time and his message of hope has encouraged Israel to survive millennia of disaster."

The Israelites, the Jews, will be brought back to their own land. In some few cases the references about God bringing his people back do have in mind the return from the exile, as Jeremiah 29:10. Generally, the reference in these passages is to a return to take place long after that. Actually the phrase is "To return a *second* time." That is what it says in Isaiah 11:11 and Jeremiah 12:15. This return will witness the Hebrew people coming back to Palestine, and here's the phrase from Jeremiah 29:14 *from all nations.* The Jews boast today that there are now Hebrew people in Palestine from 105 different countries.

They will abide in the land permanently, Jeremiah 24:6: *I will set my eyes upon them for good. I will bring them again to this land. I will build them and not pull them down. I will plant them and not pluck them up.* This has not yet taken place.

The Jews will be in their land safely. This thing of dwelling safely is frequently expressed, as in Jeremiah

33:16: *In those days shall Judah be saved? And Jerusalem shall dwell safely: and this is the name wherewith she shall be called, Jehovah, our righteousness.* Previously I referred to this matter of righteousness. It is very, very interesting that scores of prophecies concerning the future are related to this matter of righteousness. You remember Paul, preaching to the Athenian philosophers, said that when Christ came back He would judge the world "in righteousness." And the Apostle Peter, in the second of his epistles toward the end, speaks of this earth which will be renewed in righteousness (II Peter 3:13).

The Jews will again be one united nation, Ezekiel 37:15-28. Now I do not very often argue or debate with contrary opinions in this matter of eschatology. One has to teach what he believes, and let it go at that. But I must say right here, regarding this great passage of Ezekiel, that John Calvin and the great reformers for the most part were wrong when they insisted that these prophecies were going to be fulfilled in the Christian Church. Calvin said: "Whenever the prophets prophesy of the return of the people, they extended what they taught to the whole kingdom of Christ. For liberation from exile was no more than the beginning of God's favor. God began the work of true and real redemption when He restored His people to their own country. But He gave them but a slight taste of His mercy. This prophecy then with those which are like it ought to be extended to the kingdom of Christ."

In modern times, the great Old Testament scholar Keil, who saw profoundly into hundreds of passages in the Old Testament, echoes this same erroneous idea when he says: "The land which will flow like streams of divine blessing is not Palestine but the domain of the Christian Church, of the church so far as it has received the blessings of Christianity. The people who cultivate this land are the Christian church. So far as it stands a living faith."

We who are members of the Christian Church have nothing to do with the promises relating to Palestine. We don't want the land. For the most part we are not going back to that land. We are not looking for the agricultural riches of any land. We are looking for the Lord's return. We are looking for the Church to be built up and sanctified, and we are looking for heaven, the Glory of God. But the promises of Ezekiel are still true. They still relate to Israel.

You remember the Apostle Paul did something about this in the Ephesian epistle, in speaking of the great passage in the decalogue, that we were to honor our father and mother by which the Lord would give long life *in the land which the Lord thy God giveth thee.* When Paul quotes this in Ephesians he doesn't say that to these Ephesian, Greek pagans—*the land which the Lord thy God giveth thee,* he says, *that it may be well with thee, and thou mayest live long on the earth.* That is altogether a different matter. (Exodus 20:12; Ephesians 6:1-3)

Now, our third major consideration is that, *Israel will experience, a time of great trouble.* The Lord said to Jeremiah 46:28: *I will not leave thee wholly unpunished.* In Jeremiah 30:7 you have the famous phrase *The time of Jacob's trouble.* It is to this period that Moses referred when toward the close of his life he said: *Evil will befall you in the latter days,* Deuteronomy 31:29.

Jerusalem will be besieged and temporarily captured, Zechariah 14:1-3.

There will be a terrible invasion of the northern powers. Ezekiel 38-39. I believe that Russia is clearly foreseen here. In the original text the word was *rosho,* and this is Russia. It will be a tragic day for Israel.

And in that day will I make Jerusalem a burdensome stone for all people. This is most interesting, Zechariah 12:2,3. Years ago, Dr. Charles Wright wrote a great work on Zechariah in which he does not see, however, the literal fulfillment of prophecy. When he comes to Zechariah 12:3, Jerusalem will prove a burdensome stone to the nations, yet this is what he says (remember this was written 80 years ago): "In vain will the nations round about seek to fit the stone of Jerusalem into the political structures which they might seek to erect. All their efforts to raise that burdensome stone will prove injurious to themselves."

Do you realize that the city of Jerusalem, the problem of Jerusalem, has been up before the United Nations four times in the last 20 years? May I use the rough phrase, this was nothing but "a hot potato" for them. No decision was ever reached, and there is nothing being discussed on Jerusalem in the United Nations today. This is exactly what Zechariah says: It will prove a *burdensome stone* to the nations.

Now, my fourth major point is that *Israel will ultimately know a great spiritual revival.* In general you will see this in Ezekiel 37:23-28. But specifically you will find this in the 11th chapter, verses 19 and 20, which is like Jeremiah 31. May I read these beautiful words: *I will give them one heart, and I will put a new spirit within you; and I will take the stony heart out of their flesh, and will give them a heart of flesh: that they may walk in my statutes, and keep mine ordinances, and do them: and they shall be my people, and I will be their God.* These are wonderful words. They have never yet come true.

At this time the Gentile nation will come up to Jerusalem to learn the law of the Lòrd. Some of the greatest verses in the Bible relating to this subject are found in the Book of Isaiah 1:26,27 and chapter 2, verses 2 and 3.

And at the end of the Book, Isaiah doesn't seem to be able to divest himself of this theme, Isaiah 62:2,3,11,12.

Jerusalem will ultimately be ruled over by the divine son of their great King David, Jeremiah 23:5-8, and frequently in Ezekiel, such as 37:24. There is a great passage by Keil on the prophecy that Israel is to be ruled over by David. "The return to the Lord on the part of Israel cannot take place without a return to David their King. Since God has promised the kingdom to David and his seed forever," (this King David, however, is none other than the Messiah himself) "the return was not to take place till the end of the days, which does not denote the future generally but the closing future of the Kingdom of God commencing with the reign of the Messiah."

Jerusalem will ultimately be the source of Universal peace. How we need it! Isaiah 66:10-12, Haggai 2:9.

In the 9th, 10th and 11th chapters of the Epistle to the Romans, St. Paul develops his great argument concerning the ultimate salvation of these people, Israel. In chapter 9:1-3 he confesses his great love for his fellow Israelites. In verses 4 to 33 he reviews Israel's past history. And then in the 10th chapter he profoundly discusses the present condition of Israel as true today as when he wrote. And then chapter 11 begins with the great question which he is going to answer, *Hath God cast away his people?* The Apostle presents the following evidence to prove that God has not cast away His people. First Paul himself, an Israelite, was saved. Secondly, there has always been a remnant of true believers in Israel. He then develops his famous parable of two olive trees.

Israel was the true olive tree. Because of her unbelief, the original branches were broken off and they are broken off today. Gentiles are indicated by the wild olive tree. The branches of this wild tree are now grafted into the true olive tree, *contrary to nature.* Now the day will come, says the Apostle, that even these broken branches will be grafted in again to the true olive tree. So, *All Israel shall be saved* quoting Isaiah 59:20,21.

Finally, *there is a true limit to what has been determined for Israel's blindness.* This limit will be reached when the fullness of the Gentiles shall be come in. We cannot cover all the facets related to this subject. For instance, the erection of the Temple in Jerusalem, which must take place before Daniel 12:11 and Matthew 24:15 and II Thessalonians 2:3,4 can take place. This is the Temple referred to in Revelation 11:1-10. See also Deuteronomy 28:62.

Because of her great tribulation the time will come when the Jews will be few in number. This is an interesting statement in Isaiah 27:6 *That Israel shall blossom and bud, and fill the face of the world with fruit.* And at the end of Zephaniah 3:19 we read, *I will get them praise and fame in every land where they have been put to shame.* This concludes, with much left undiscussed, our survey of prophecies relating to Israel.

CHAPTER 5

The Antichrist, Master of Deception

From the beginning of history, and, as to Satan and the fallen angels, even before human history, there have always been individuals and organized groups of individuals opposed to God, to Christ, to the Word of God and the people of God. Some have been and are mere human beings, though demon-controlled, such as the pharaoh of the oppression. Antiochus Epiphanes, Judas Iscariot, Julian the apostate—false christs and false prophets.

At certain epochal times these enemies of God organized in large groups to carry out their evil programs, such as the armies depicted in Ezekiel 38 and 39, or the ten kings of one mind who make war with the Lamb, in Revelation 17:12-18. Some of these opponents of God's plan to redeem men and establish universal righteousness are supernatural beings—as the fallen angels, the principalities and powers in heavenly places, evil spirits, demons, etc. and particularly Satan —sometimes called the Devil, the Serpent and the great Dragon, as in Revelation 12:9.

In the Book of Revelation, apart from Satan, the two most important enemies of God are the Beast out of the sea and the Beast out of the earth. Now before we look at Antichrist himself, who is yet to come, we should consider for a moment some earlier references to some outstanding enemies of God. We will not be able to comment on these in detail.

In Daniel 7:8,19-26, is revealed the little horn who makes war with the saints and speaks great words against the Most High. Note here the emphasis on the *mouth*, in verses 8, 20 and 25. This will reappear in the discussion of Antichrist in Revelation 13:2-6. And notice the chronological limitation here of Daniel 7, *Until a time, times, and the dividing of times,* exactly as in Revelation 12:14.

Then in the next chapter, Daniel 8:23-27, there is the king of fierce countenance who is to appear in the latter time typified by that great enemy of the Jews, Antiochus Epiphanes.

Then at the end of the book in Daniel 11:36-45; 12:1, we read of *The king who speaks against the God of gods.*

But we must consider, however, in more detail this man of sin, Antichrist, in St. Paul's writings. Unless we consider the one referred to in John 5:43 as Antichrist, there is no reference to such a person in the teachings of Jesus. But St. Paul has a tremendously important passage on this subject in the second epistle which he wrote to the Thessalonians, chapter 2, verses 3-10. Here Antichrist is depicted as *the man of sin.* I am quoting, (Who) *as God sitteth in the temple of God, showing himself that he is God.* And in verse 8 he is referred to literally as *the lawless one.* Which brings back to our mind the reference which we saw in a preceding chapter to great lawlessness at the end of this age. This lawless one will be energized by Satan. He will produce signs and lying wonders. Dr. John Eadie, one of the great biblical scholars of a former generation, has a good comment here. "This unparalleled hallucination," that is, he will deceive many who will believe a lie, "This unparalleled hallucination indicates a mysterious state of mind and of society, antichristian, antitheistic, credulous with a fatal facility of being imposed upon by diabolical mystery and subtlety."

Eighty years ago Dr. William G. Moorehead, one of the great American biblical scholars, an editor of the First Edition of the *Scofield Reference Bible,* wrote some remarkable words regarding this man of sin. "This one, this lawless one, is the one in whom all law is discarded." (And by the way, this was written before our century and how appropriate this is for the lawless day in which we are living.) "All moral order is dethroned. Upon the ruins of shattered states and kingdoms the vast empire of Antichrist is built. The revolutionary condition of society" (this is very, very important—this is before Communism, before the First World War) "out of which the Antichrist and his dominion arise is clearly indicated by Daniel 7:2 where it says that the four winds of heaven break upon the great sea and the beasts arose. Out of the same unstable and agitated elements the beast of the Apocalypse comes forth. The sea torn by the wind is the graphic image of nations and peoples in commotion and revolution. History affords at least one illustrious example of the malignant process through which the world will travel to the man of sin. That is the French Revolution. Is this to be the final outcome of the boasted progress of civilization of our modern era? The science, discoveries, culture, the energy, activity and splendid achievement of the age—are they all to terminate in worldwide godlessness and the man of sin? This view may be called pessimistic and those holding it may be called pessimists, but He whose love for men is deathless, whose power is matchless, Himself said, *As it was in the days of Noah, so shall it be in the days of the Son of man.* How was it in the days of Noah? The world was in revolt against God." (See Genesis 6:5-13).

Now we pass from the Apostle Paul to the Apostle John. Actually the word antichrist appears only in St. John's epistles, though the person of Antichrist is often elsewhere referred to under names as we have already seen. This is in I John, chapter 2, verses 18-22; chapter 4, verse 3; and II John 7. These are the verses in which the word actually appears. Here he that denies Jesus is the Antichrist, he denies the Father and the Son. Note that in II John 7 we have what we referred to previously, this factor of deception. The great New Testament scholar, Candlish, commenting on the deeper aspects of this sobering theme once wrote: "The denial of the fact that Jesus is the Christ, when grasped in its full significance, intellectual, moral, spiritual includes all falsehood. It takes away the highest ideal of sacrifice. It destroys the connection of God and man."

Now for the third division. First in St. Paul, then in St. John, now in the Book of Revelation. The most important single chapter regarding Antichrist in the Bible is Revelation 13. Here two beasts are depicted—one out of the sea, verses 1-10, and the other out of the earth, verses 11-18. This second beast causes men to worship the first beast, and to make an image of the first beast, thus implying that the first beast was the more important.

It is this first beast who is referred to elsewhere in

the book of Revelation as the beast coming up out of the sea—chapter 13, verses 1-10. It is also referred to as the first beast in 15:2; 16:10; 17:17; 19:19. So really this makes five different passages in which this first beast is referred to in the Book of Revelation—from chapter 13 to the end of chapter 19. It is his mark, the mark of the first beast, that will be stamped on his followers, chapter 16:2; 19:20; 20:4. Twice the two beasts are referred to as the beast and the false prophet, Revelation 16:13; 20:10. In these two passages Satan himself is included.

Now the first beast whose horns and diadems represent power, is energized by Satan. It is almost unbelievable but here is what the scriptures say, that the whole earth will worship both the beast and the dragon. There will be much religion on earth in the latter days, but it will be godless and blasphemous.

All this reminds us of the second chapter of Daniel, where the great Babylonian king made all of his officers bow down to the image that was erected and worship that image. What you have on a minor, limited, geographical scale in Babylon, in the days of Daniel, you will have on a universal scale at the end of this age.

The first beast, now notice his characteristics, is against God. He is satanically energized. He is supreme in military matters. He possesses world-wide power and persecutes the saints of the earth.

We are too prone today, being occupied with the war in southeast Asia, with ecology—cleaning up the rivers and lakes, etc., all of which is very, very important—to forget that Russia and all of the communistic countries and practically all of China, with perhaps 800 million people, and all of North Korea and all of the other communistic countries are anti-God. They are anti-Christ. We must not forget that there are hundreds of millions of people living under certain governments today where the governments themselves deny the reality of God and repudiate the Lord Jesus.

From 1890 to 1910, when we felt we were moving toward a millenium and universal peace, this idea that nations would be godless was inconceivable. But it is a reality today. This means that the world is setting a stage for the very things which are predicted in the thirteenth chapter of the Book of Revelation.

While the first beast is undoubtedly a political world power, the second beast, as Lee has said, is a spiritual world power—a power of learning and knowledge, of ideas, of intellectual cultivation. Both are from below. Both are beasts. Both are in close alliance.

"The worldly anti-Christian wisdom stands in the service of the worldly anti-Christian power." This is from Professor Lee who wrote one of the great commentaries on the Book of Revelation, about 1870. "The worldly anti-Christian wisdom"—what does he mean by that? Well, this means the professorial chairs in our universities, especially in philosophy, that are occupied by unbelievers. And most of the chairs of philosophy in our country are occupied by men who do not believe in a personal God. This refers to the great mass of literature that is published by members of the French Academy and elsewhere. I would say that 95 percent of these writers are unbelievers. This is what Lee means by "worldly anti-Christian wisdom."

I am sorry to say that a great majority of the leading scientists of the modern world are not theistic. While they might not be anti-God, they at least have eliminated God from their thinking and from their teaching.

The second beast enforces the commands of the first beast and accompanies his evil work with various forms of miraculous manifestations. The period of the time of the gentiles began with this forced worship that I mentioned before, and this period will close with a similar forced worship on a universal scale.

There is one theme that underlies all the work of Satan and of Antichrist, and that is *deception.* I want to emphasize this. Even Eve acknowledged that Satan had deceived her, Genesis 3:13. The Apostle reaffirmed it in I Timothy 2:14. Deception is referred to in our Lord's great prophetic discourse four times in Matthew 24, verses 4 and 5 and 11 and 24. The false prophet in Revelation 13, 14, 19, 20 is characterized by this activity of deception. To me one of the most terrible statements in all the Bible is in Revelation 12:9 where we read *Satan . . . deceiveth the whole world.* And I would say that antitheistic men and women, those who are anti-God, those who are atheistic, those who are anti-Christ—that is, who are against the truth —they are believing a lie.

On the matter of a single world government, for which many men have been agitating for decades, and never more persistently than now, which is the kind of a government this chapter speaks of—may I here quote the statement of one of the great scientists of our generation. He is famous both in physics and in astronomy, Dr. Harold C. Urey, for many years professor at the University of Chicago—now, at the University of California, La Jolla. When at the time of the development and the explosion of the atomic bomb he warned us, "Regarding giving the secrets of to a world government" (that is the secrets of the atomic power) "such a super world government is not a solution to world power. For there is the possibility that a tyrant will get control of the world through this instrument of atomic energy. The atomic bomb is characteristic of a tyrant's weapon." (This is a professor speaking now.) "It is just the weapon that would enable a dictator to sit firmly in his seat and no one could do anything about it." And this reminds us of that passage in the early part of Revelation 13, *Who is able to make war with him?* That is, he would have such military power that no one could make war against him. This is exactly what Urey says. May I repeat, "This is just the weapon that would enable a dictator to sit firmly in his seat and no one could do anything about it."

More than a century ago Dr. Carl August Auberlen, the distinguished theologian, published one of the profoundest books of prophecy of the 19th century which was called *Daniel and Revelation*. I would like to quote the following sober lines, much of which we have seen has come true since Auberlen wrote them.

"The apostasy will commence in a way which will be imperceptable to most people. It will have an appearance of Christianity in its outward form, as there were weeds which looked like wheat. But by degrees the more the apostasy spreads, the more powerful it becomes in numbers and worldly influence. It will unfold with increasing distinctness its anti-Christian character and finally betray, sell and persecute the people. The false prophet asserts that the forms and documents of Christianity are of no importance. This is exactly what we are hearing today—that everything depends on fundamental ideas under which spacious pretext he gets rid of everything in Christianity. When we are told that the false prophet breathes spirit into the image that speaks, this is a striking description of the fact that the false doctrine is capable of giving a spiritual, rational, philosophical appearance to the foolish idolatry and apotheosis of the creature. This is the new heathenism sunk back into the deification of nature and humanity. It is evident and it is palpable that the philosophic principle of the autonomy of the human spirit and the theological principle of rationalism and materialism and atheism are the products of this same spirit, the essence of which is falling away—is apostasy from the fundamental principles of Christianity. Alienation from the living and holy God—deification of the creaturely—this is what is meant in the apocalypse by the worship of the beast. And are we not worshipping man today and all that belongs to man and all the achievements of man, even the bodies of men? What is bringing thousands from Christianity? And preventing others from coming to a belief in a full Christianity? Nothing else but a respect for these so-called intellectual powers which rule in these days for modern science and culture." This was written in 1860. The worst thing is that scarcely anyone sees the danger of this evil.

From the earliest apostolic writers down to this generation, Antichrist has been identified, but wrongly, with the Roman Empire, with Judas Iscariot raised from the dead, or Nero. The reformers, even Luther and Calvin, identified Antichrist with the papacy, which is wrong. Many believed it was Napoleon Bonaparte or Napoleon III, and in this century some said it was Mussolini or Hitler. All these guesses are wrong. We wait yet for *the* Antichrist to appear on the stage of history.

Even at the beginning of the 3rd Century there was a great early Christian theologian by the name of Hippolytus who wrote an entire treatise on Christ and Antichrist. So this is not a new subject that we are introducing here that the churches never heard of before. The Church began to hear of Antichrist from the very beginning.

CHAPTER 6

He's Coming Again!

Of all the so-called world religions such as Buddhism, Shintoism, Confucianism and Mohammedanism, Christianity is the only one that has for one of its basic teachings the return of its founder to this earth. It is the cardinal theme even in the short Apostles' Creed where we read: *He ascended into heaven and sitteth on the right hand of God the Father Almighty from thence He shall come to judge the quick and the dead.* The Athanasian Creed adds, *At whose advent all men are to rise again with their bodies and render an account of their own deeds.*

The leading authority today on the early creeds of the church, Professor J. N. D. Kelly, of England, affirms of early Christians that, "It was the promise of His coming to judge the living and the dead which loomed largest and most impressive in the catechumen's consciousness."

Before entering into an examination of the New Testament teaching about this hope-begetting doctrine, we should remind ourselves of four elemental matters.

First, there is to be only one return of Christ after His ascension. That is, the church speaks about the second advent, never the third advent nor the fourth advent, only the *second*. This second advent ends this age and establishes Christ's reign upon earth.

Second, this event is still future. To identify it with the fall of Jerusalem, or any other past event, or with the death of the believer, has no scriptural justification whatever.

Third, we should not forget that this Person of whose advent we are here speaking is the one whose first advent was of such profound and universal significance, that even all the dates now, of ancient and modern history, are determined by this advent—this first advent. It was in His first advent that by His resurrection He gave men a hope that does not fade away but will be consummated in our resurrection and glory. It was because of His first advent and ministry on earth that the church of Christ is now made possible. Finally, we are to remember that the second advent is exclusively concerned with *this* earth on which the human race exists. It is not a second appearance on some other planet, but a coming back to this earth, on which our redemption was wrought out in the first half of the first century of our era.

The word *advent* implies of course a "coming to" and this has for a necessary corollary a "coming from." Christ was received up into heaven at the time of His ascension and He will in His second advent return from heaven, Acts 1:11 and I Thessalonians 4:16. This may be the place to state that there are a number of passages in the Gospels that are definitely eschatological in their teaching but in which there are no specific references to Christ's return, even though in some it may be implied; as for instance, Matthew 10:14,15 and Matthew 11:20-24. Even the great statement at the Lord's Supper, *Until I drink it new with you in my Father's kingdom,* is eschatological, but there is nothing here specific about His return.

There are four words in the Greek New Testament which are used to indicate the second advent of Christ, the commonest of which is *parousia*. In the Latin it is the word *adventus*, from which is derived our word, "advent." This word is used by St. Paul in reference to the coming of Antichrist, but generally to the second coming of our Lord. Then there is the word *ephiphanea* which means appearance, out of which comes our word "epiphany." A third word is *apocalypsis* which means "revelation," from which comes our word "apocalypse." Finally, there is the ordinary verb "to come," to arrive with somebody, coming to someone's home, or coming to a city. This is *erkomai*.

The second advent of Christ is not referred to in any other but one of these four words. All of these words are sometimes used to refer to the first advent as well as to the second advent! Thus, no one word in the Greek New Testament refers exclusively to the second advent. Nor is any one of these four when transposed into the English languages used exclusively for the second advent. All efforts to distinguish various periods of the second advent, as supposedly designated by these separate words have not proved satisfactory.

In our study of our Lord's second advent we find some phenomena that are arresting. Notice Matthew 24:30,31: *Then shall appear the sign of the Son of man in heaven*: now watch carefully, *then shall all the tribes of the earth mourn, and they shall see the Son of man coming in the clouds of heaven with power and great glory. And he shall send his angels with a great sound of a trumpet.* Here you have clouds of heaven, power, great glory and angels. You have four phenomena here. Three of these phenomena occur in the marvelous passages in the Book of Exodus when God is about to meet with Moses or His people, in a thick cloud over the tabernacle, and also on Mount Sinai, Exodus 19:16; Exodus 34:5; Exodus, chapter 40, verses 34 and 35. In other words, this second advent of our Lord will be accompanied by those phenomena which were present when God revealed Himself on particular occasions to His people Israel. Of course this word *power* is very significant. He was crucified with weakness; He was raised with power (II Corinthians 13:4). He subjected Himself to the verdicts of the rulers of this earth the first time, but when He comes the second time He will subdue all the powers of the world, human and satanic; He will then exercise omnipotence in every realm of this world. He will reign with undisputed authority.

In the definitive passage in Paul's first letter to the Thessalonians, one of the greatest passages on the second advent in the New Testament, another group of phenomena is particularly emphasized. We read in I Thessalonians 4:16, *The Lord himself shall descend from heaven with a shout, with the voice of the archangel, and with the trump of God: and the dead in Christ shall rise first.* The word translated "shout" is frequently used in classical Greek of a command in battle. It is not stated by whom the shout in the present instance is uttered. Perhaps by an archangel, more probably by the Lord Himself, as the principal subject of the entire sentence.

We must consider for a few moments a subject about which many books have been written, yet about which there has been considerable confusion, even today, concerning which we want to be very, very careful. I refer to the sequence of events to occur when Christ returns. No student can be expected to construct a chronology, even of only the main prophetic events to be introduced by the return of our Lord that will satisfy everyone. One aspect over which opinions vary widely is the millennium. Many in the church, true believers, reject the whole concept of the millennium and the rule of Christ on this earth. I think Calvin himself had nothing to do with the millennium. Other Christians who do believe in a millennium are divided into two groups—those who look for the Church to bring about a millennium preceding Christ's return, and those who consider a millennial era possible only when Christ returns. Of those holding this latter view that it will be Christ who introduces the millennium, some believe that Christ may come at any time, others that the Church must go through some period of tribulation, and still others that the Church at the end of the age must go through the entire tribulation after which the Lord will return. Some give no place at all to a future existence of Israel on this earth, others believe that the unfulfilled Old Testament prophecies of Israel are still valid.

Now, before we consider the major events connected with our Lord's return, let us recall six passages in the New Testament that set forth a series of events—that is a sort of calendar of prophecy. This is fundamental to the Olivet Discourse which, as we noticed before, speaks of three eras—before the tribulation, during the tribulation, after the tribulation. Then there are the two summaries of prophetic events in the classic statement of Paul about the resurrection in I Corinthians 15. I Thessalonians 4:15-17 sets the well-known summary of events relating to the rapture of believers at the time of the second advent.

In II Thessalonians 2:2-12 there is unfolded another *series* of future events in relation to the view of Antichrist.

Finally, on almost the last page of the scriptures, Revelation 20:1-12, we have a series of eight events to follow after the Battle of Armageddon down to the very last judgment. Now every event that will occur as a result of our Lord's return must be assigned to some period, some place in the sequence of events. Let me state again: every event that is to occur at the time of our Lord's return must be assigned its proper place within the framework of these six passages. And this is a problem.

Now let's talk about some of these events. First, the resurrection of believers and the translation of the Church. The resurrection of believers who have died, as Milligan has said, will be the first in the great drama of the second advent, to be followed by the rapture of the living saints. To my own mind the resurrection of our bodies involves just about the greatest exercise of divine power displayed in any event in the history of the universe. In some ways it seems even greater than creation itself. This is the hope continually set forth by the apostles as in I Corinthians 6:14,15 and I Peter 1:3,4—you remember those wonderful words, (Who) *hath begotten us again unto a lively hope by the resurrection of Jesus Christ from the dead.* This is worked out in great detail in the 15th chapter of I Corinthians. There is no question about it, all believers will be involved in this. This is what we may call the completion, the final completion of our salvation, culminating in our entrance into glory.

Second, there is the judgment of believers. At this time there will be a careful reckoning of what believers have done while on earth, II Corinthians 5:10, *Whether it be good or bad.* And in Colossians 3:24, *Of the Lord ye shall receive the reward of the inheritance.*

It is probably here that we should introduce the theme of *reward,* so frequently referred to by our Lord in six of His great parables: the parables of men who wait for the Lord, Luke 12:35-40; the parable of the faithful and wise steward, Luke 12:41-48; the parable of the right and wrong use of what has been committed to us, Luke 19:11-17; the parable of the wicked husbandmen and the owner of the vineyard, Luke 20:9-16; (the only one of these parables in all three of the synoptics) that of the wise and foolish virgins, Matthew 25:1-13; and the talents, same chapter, verses 14-30.

We ought to look at this second advent for a moment as the ground and foundation of our hope. Down through the ages the Church has always referred to the second advent of the Lord as the great hope of believers. St. Paul in Titus 2:13 calls it *that blessed hope.* In fact, the second advent of our Lord is involved in all the important New Testament passages that refer in any way to the Christian's hope. Sometimes it is designated *the hope of glory* (Colossians 1:27); sometimes *the hope of eternal life* (Titus 1:2); sometimes the *hope of righteousness* (Galatians 5:5). St. Paul speaks in Colossians 1:5 of *the hope which is laid up for you in heaven.* In the well-known passage at the beginning of his first Epistle, St. Peter reminds us that God, according to His great mercy hath begotten us unto this living hope, that we are to be raised incorruptible, undefiled in a body that fadeth not away, reserved in heaven for us who are kept by the power of God (I Peter 1:3-5). It is significant that in the writings of the Apostle Paul alone, the noun "hope" appears twenty-eight times and in verbal form twenty-one times. How pitiful to present any other hope than that of the Lord's return to our sick world.

How strange the hopes of the early twentieth century now sound. For example, the famous speech of Woodrow Wilson before the United States Senate, in July 1919, which he called "The Hope of the World," by which he had in mind the League of Nations while, of course, there is no League of Nations today. Or the statement of the Chief Justice of the United States Supreme Court, Charles Evans Hughes, on February, 1927, at the end of the Disarmament Conference, when he gave the verdict (I'm quoting Justice Hughes), "This treaty, February, 1927, ends, absolutely ends, the race in competition in naval armament."

Now having quoted Woodrow Wilson and Chief Justice Hughes, may I come to more modern times. Only a few weeks ago I received an address sent to me from the White House (I do not know why, but I get one perhaps every two months or so), by the man who has just retired as a close counselor of the President, who is now returning to Harvard University. It was a great and inspiring address on a very high level. But he ended by saying that America was the hope of the world! Now this is exactly what Woodrow Wilson was saying. America, the hope of the world. With all of our crime and sin and everything else that we have to contend with, we are the hope of the world? The only hope of this world, and I'm no pessimist, is for the Lord to return in power. The hope for the defeat of Communism is in the return of the Lord. The hope of cleansing this earth of its pain and sin and crime, and the restoration of righteousness, is in the return of the Lord Jesus Christ. This is the only hope worth holding and embracing and proclaiming. This is the one hope that is certainly going to come true by the power of God.

Now we might ask a question: When will Christ return? In His great prophetic discourse on the Mount of Olives Jesus declared that *of that day and hour knoweth no man, no, not the angels of heaven, but my Father only*. Later in the discourse He repeated these words several times. Yet despite these and similar warnings, some men in every age of the church have foolishly attempted to construct chronological schemes of future events with dates attached. I have about thirty books in my library, each of which predicts the year in which the Lord will return and each is different, and all these dates are already in the past. These schemes are invariably futile. They only confirm the impossibility of arriving at any chronological conclusion of this age from the data of the scriptures. We do not know the *year* of our Lord's return.

On the other hand, there are such things as signs of the times. Christ after enumerating various phenomena that would occur between His first and second advent and especially toward the end of this age, exhorted his disciples with these words: *Ye, when ye shall see all these things, know that it is near, even at the doors* (Matthew 24:33). Now, to be sure, many distinguished servants of God down through the ages have felt convinced that they were living at the end of the age. This belief was expressed as early as the fourth century by Lactanius. In the Middle Ages there was a great literature known as the *Fifteen Signs Before Doomsday*. Martin Luther commenting on Luke 21 went into great detail as to his own convictions that he then was at the end of the age. And there have been and are modern writers with the same persuasion. Their error does not however prevent us from considering some of the *phenomena* that the New Testament says will mark the end of the age.

Concerning many of the signs of the times to be witnessed at the end of the age, we should carefully consider the Olivet Discourse. While on the one hand we do not know exactly when Christ will return, many today, and many more now than a half a century ago, are convinced that unless we should be granted a great world wide revival, the stage is being set for the great climax of history when our Lord Jesus will return. This great flood of lawlessness has prophetic significance of course. And so does Israel's return to Palestine. But I do not think that it can yet be said we are actually in *the* apostasy, though the godlessness of Communism has its significance.

Now one word about the life we are to live as we look for our Lord's return. Most of all, the Apostle emphasizes holy living. *What manner of persons ought ye to be?* (II Peter 3:11). Then there should be faithfulness in serving the Lord which we have referred to in the parables we mentioned a moment ago. There should be the virtue of patience—waiting patiently for the Lord to come (James 5:7,8). There is a beautiful clause in II Timothy 4:8, *We are to love His appearing.* I remember once the great Bible teacher, George Guille, now in heaven, began a series of meetings in a Presbyterian church in the South whose minister he had never met before. Before they went in to the first service on that Sunday night, George Guille, in his gracious and lovely southern way, said to the minister, "Do you love His appearing?" And I think we might ask ourselves this.

CHAPTER 7

Armageddon

The Old Testament historical narratives are saturated with the subject of war. From the 14th chapter of Genesis down to the destruction of Jerusalem by Nebuchadnezzar there are approximately one hundred different military events, battles, sieges and wars—most of which involved Israel and Judah! In addition, there are a number of predictions about wars to occur in centuries to follow.

The New Testament is practically free from this theme, apart from the Book of Revelation, with the single exception of our Lord's predictions concerning the coming destruction of Jerusalem, and His general statement at the beginning of the Olivet Discourse about wars and rumors of wars, (Matthew 24:6,7). The fall of

Jerusalem occurred under the Roman general Titus in A.D. 70. Strange to say, though some books in the New Testament were written after A.D. 70, an actual account of the destruction of Jerusalem as predicted by Jesus is not to be found in the New Testament. The Book of Revelation reveals repeated conflicts of a military nature terminating in the great battle of Armageddon in the 19th chapter. To this we must turn.

Indeed the word Armageddon itself has come to mean, as the great *Oxford English Dictionary* tells us, "The place of the last decisive battle at the day of judgment, hence used illustratively for any final conflict on a great scale." This reminds me that even the great scholars who put together this famous *Oxford English Dictionary* are not too well acquainted with Biblical eschatology. Notice this phrase, "The last decisive battle at the day of judgment." It will be the last decisive battle, but it will be a long, long way from the day of judgment.

There will be a great battle at the end of the age between Christ and Antichrist predicted in the Old Testament, as in Joel 3:9-15; Jeremiah 51:27-36 and Zephaniah 3:8. While the battle of Armageddon in itself is only described in Revelation 19:11-21, it is referred to as a coming event in three places in the Book of Revelation before the battle is actually described, Revelation 14:14-20; 16:16-16; 17:8-17. So much for general predictions of the battle.

The Greek word Armageddon means "the mount of Magedon." The word *Magedon* comes from a root *Gadad* meaning "to cut off," that is, "slaughter." *Megiddo* refers to an ancient city west of the Jordan, northeast of Mount Carmel overlooking a vast plain known generally as the Plain of Jezreel or the Plain of Esdraelon. The word *Megiddo* occurs in the Old Testament often. Joshua 12:21; 17:11; Judges 5:19; I Kings

4:12; II Kings 9:27-30; I Chronicles 7:29; II Chronicles 35:22; Zechariah 12:11.

A well-known authority on biblical geography wrote this about the Plain of Esdraelon, "Properly regarded," he said, "this is triangular in shape from Mount Tabor in the north by way of the slopes of little Hermon to the foothills of Mount Gilboa. From Gilboa to the base of Mount Carmel where the low hills of Galilee form a narrow pass at the entrance to the Plain of Acre. From Carmel by way of the southern Galilean steps to Mount Tabor. Now these lines, of course, are irregular, but they, in general, represent the limits of the Plains from Tabor to Gilboa, the distance of fourteen miles. From Gilboa to Carmel the distance is twenty-four miles, and from Carmel to Tabor, fourteen miles.

"The area thus enclosed is justly regarded as one of the most beautiful plains in the world. Of strategic importance, this plain lies across the path of all approaches to central and southern Canaan to the north." Someone has said, "It is the only plain, the only level ground in all of Palestine where a million soldiers could be maneuvered."

Some of the greatest battles of history, especially in Israel's history have been fought here. First the Battle of Barak over the Moabites of which we read in Judges 5:20, *The stars in their courses fought against Sisera.* That is, it seemed that nature itself was against the Moabites. Second, the battle of Gideon and his three hundred men and their victory over the Midianites (Judges 7). Third, the terrible defeat of the Israelites by the Philistines, involving the death of Saul and his sons (I Samuel 31). Fourth, at Megiddo, King Josiah was slain by Pharaoh Necho of Egypt (II Kings 23:29,30). Fifth, Edmund H. Allenby, in 1918, turned the Turkish army and saved the Near East for the Western allies. For this reason, because of his great victory, there on the Plain of Megiddo he was given the permanent title of honor, Field Marshall Lord Allenby of Megiddo. I can remember back in 1918, and many years after that, during which we had extensive literature proving that Armageddon had been fought, that Allenby's victory over the Turkish people was the fulfillment of Revelation 19. Don't you believe it, not a word of it! This was not the Battle of Armageddon, though it was fought on the plains where that great battle will be. The Battle of Armageddon will be between Christ and the forces arrayed against Him—the kingdoms of the earth. This was not true of Allenby's defeat of the Turks in 1918.

At the mound of Megiddo which lifts high above this plain, the University of Chicago for many, many years carried on extensive excavations. They found fourteen different civilizations. The entire mound has never been fully excavated. Much remains to be done but from that mountain you can get a marvelous view, the greatest view in Palestine, of the plain on which this battle will be fought. It is most interesting that it is right here at Megiddo where occurred the first battle of which we have any extensive record. Let me quote now from a book entitled *The Battle of Megiddo* by the famous Egyptologist Harold Nelson, published by the University of Chicago in 1913. He is not talking about a future battle, he is talking about an ancient battle. "The battle of Megiddo," says Nelson after excavating this mound, "on May 15, 1479 B.C. under Thutmose III," this is an Egyptian king, "and the allied forces of the Serbian states is the first battle in history which we can study in any detail the military maneuvers and tactics. It is the first battle in history in which in any measure we can study the disposition of troops, and as such it forms the starting point for the history of military science." This is very interesting. If ancient

Megiddo is the starting point for the history of military science, then Megiddo in the end of this age will be the end of military science and military maneuvers.

One of the most remarkable paragraphs regarding Megiddo is in that marvelous work by George Adam Smith, *The Historical Geography of the Holy Land,* which went through about thirty-five editions. To anyone interested in literature regarding the geography of the Bible, this is the one indispensable work. Many have followed since, many are important, many have new things in them that George Adam Smith didn't know. Here is what he wrote: "What a plain it is, upon which not only the greatest empires, races and faiths of east and west have contended with each other, but each has come to judgment. On which from the first with all its splendor of human battle, men have felt that there was fighting from heaven—the stars in their courses were fighting, upon which panic has descended so mysteriously upon the best equipped and the most successful armies. But the humble have been exalted to victory in the hour of their weakness. On which false faiths, (that's Mohammedanism which won the great battle at the Horns of Hatton, you remember, under Saladin), equally with false defenders of the faith (this would be the Crusaders), have been exposed and scattered. On which from the time of Saul willfulness and superstition, though aided by every human excellence, have come to naught. And since Josiah's time, the purest piety has not atoned for rash and mistaken zeal." I repeat these lines, "On which from the first, with all of its splendor of human battle, men have felt that there was fighting from heaven, the stars in their courses were fighting . . . and false faiths equally with false defenders of the faith have been exposed and scattered."

Now we have done three things so far. That is, we

have talked about war in the Bible in general; we have presented some general predictions of the Battle of Armageddon, Old Testament and New Testament; and we have noticed the location and significance of this Plain of Megiddo. Finally, we call attention to the person of the Lord Jesus Christ in this event.

At the beginning of the account of the Battle of Armageddon, Christ is referred to as *the faithful and true who in righteousness doth judge and make war.* This phrase, *in righteousness,* is important. Judgment throughout the Bible is always identified with righteousness. This is exactly the phrase used by the Apostle Paul in his famous statement to the Athenian philosophers when he said, When Christ would return *He will judge the world in righteousness by that man whom He hath ordained* (Acts 17:31). In fact this is the word used in the first reference to God as the judge of all the earth in Genesis 18:25; and Psalm 9:4,8 and Isaiah 11:4. This is in the form of a question. *Shall not the judge of all the earth do right?* "Righteousness" says the great authority, Cremer, "is that divine standard which shows itself in behavior conformable to God." The righteousness that men are to display corresponds with divine righteousness.

The description of the Lord in Revelation 19:12,13 tells us of one with eyes like a flame of fire and of garments sprinkled with blood. This takes us back to the beginning of the book, chapter 1, verse 14 and chapter 2, verse 18. The phrase "sprinkled with blood" is from Isaiah 63:3.

We should now notice something very significant in this Armageddon battle. Christ now is assigned the tremendous title, *the Word of God.* You remember that John opens his Gospel by saying, *In the beginning was the Word, and the Word was with God, and the Word was God.* And then in verse 14 he says: *And the Word was made flesh and dwelt among us.* Here you have that same title coming up in Revelation 19:13. The One coming down from heaven to fight the Battle of Armageddon is the Word of God. He is the Word of God who made the world. It is by rejection of the Word that sin was brought into the world. By the Word of God salvation is offered to men. Sin and anarchy, godlessness and rebellion in one way or another result from the repudiation of the Word of God. That Word, eternal, omnipotent, now descends from heaven to fulfill prophecy—to destroy the enemies of God—to reveal to the universe once and forever the folly of resisting Christ, and the indisputable pre-eminence of the King of kings and the Lord of lords.

Finally, note how quickly this battle is over. Just a couple of verses, in fact, just a couple of lines. I have seen books of a thousand pages on the Battle of Waterloo, and there are scores of books written on the great battles of the First World War and the Second World War. There is no discussion of battle here at all. There is no tension. There is no delay in the overwhelming defeat of these powerful forces gathered from the ends of the earth. They seem to be smitten at once; the Beast and the False Prophet are seized and cast into the lake of fire and brimstone. Just this little word, "caught up"—lifted up—and then "cast" is an indication of the enormous power of the omnipotence of the Lord as He comes down to deal with the antagonistic nations of the earth.

Now a word regarding the preparation of the world for this event. It is not necessary to present events bearing testimony to the tragic increase of military activity, and vast military expenditures in this 20th century. Let me give you a comment from what is in many ways the greatest single commentary on the Book of Revelation in our language. This is on the Greek text, written by Dr. Henry Barclay Swete, who for many years was professor at Cambridge University. This was in 1906, *before* the First World War, when the whole world was filled with sunshine, and we thought we were on the verge of international and permanent peace. Here is what a great scholar can draw out of the Book of Revelation long before any events are taking place that would seem to prepare for this. "As the Lamb Christ is followed by the saints but as the celestial warrior coming from heaven to bring to earth a mission of judgment He takes with Him His angels. Whereas their captain is arrayed in a cloak sprinkled with blood, they are clad in pure white. He only has had experienced of mortal conflict, for them bloodshed and death were impossible. The course of the battle is not recorded; its issue is stated: The Beast, the prime mover in the revolt against the King of kings when the day was manifestly lost, made an effort to escape but his flight was interrupted and he was seized by the Lord. This prediction seems to point to the vast struggle between society and the Church or rather between Christ and Antichrist. Those who take note of the tendencies of modern civilization will not find it impossible to conceive that a time may come when throughout Christendom the spirit of Antichrist will, with the support of the State" (this is tremendously important, a professor in a quiet atmosphere of a great university looking into the Book of Revelation even in a day of universal peace and writing this), "make a final stand against a Christianity which is loyal to the person and the teaching of Christ. The Battle of Armageddon may be considered as the final manifestation of the spirit of rebellion set forth in the II Psalm."

Finally, as to the enemies of God, the Beast and the False Prophet are cast into hell. These are the first two individuals to enter into that awful and eternal place.

The Devil is not yet cast into hell, but into a bottomless pit. There follows then a brief description of the millenial reign of Christ. Here is fulfilled the words of Isaiah 2:4, *He shall judge among the nations, and shall rebuke many people; and they shall beat their swords into plowshares, and their spears into pruning hooks: then after Armageddon nation shall not lift up sword against nation, neither shall they learn war anymore.*

CHAPTER 8

The Resurrection

When a Christian utters the two theme-related clauses of the Apostle's Creed, "I believe in Jesus Christ who the third day rose from the dead" and "I believe in the resurrection of the body," he confesses the absolute uniqueness and the supernaturalness of the person of Jesus Christ, and the glorious hope which Christ has brought to men. No other world religion has ever framed a confession embracing such truths as these, though some religions vaguely affirm belief in immortality in one form or another. Judaism in its orthodox affirmations may even give expression to the idea of a future bodily resurrection, but none ever hints that its founders, either Abraham or Moses had, in the point of time on this earth, come forth from a tomb in a resurrection body.

Whatever be the rich legacy of the great thinkers in cultures of the ancient world, they have left no contribution to the doctrine of the resurrection of the body. Such an impartial work as the great *Oxford English Dictionary* wholly ignores Osiris and the rituals of Osiris, Greek myths, Zoroastrian speculation, passes all these by and gives the first definition of the word "resurrection" as follows: "The rising again of Christ after his death and burial." This bears witness to the uniqueness of this event in world history.

Toynbee's treatment of the resurrection of Christ in his epochal study of history is most significant. One chapter is devoted to the subject of so called correspondences between the story of Jesus and the stories of certain Hellenic saviours, but in this attempt at a parallel tabulation, Toynbee lists 87 events and aspects of Christ for which he says parallels can be found in the stories of the heroes of antiquity, beginning with the hero of royal lineage, etc. But there is no hint that in the ancient world there is a story worth placing at the side of the New Testament account of the resurrection of Christ. Toynbee does not believe in the resurrection of Christ, but it is interesting that he does not dare consider anything as parallel to this supernatural event.

In the four Gospels there are 57 different references to the resurrection and the resurrection of Christ, embracing 172 verses. In Acts there are 21 separate passages totaling 43 verses. In the Epistles of Paul there are 36 references totaling 54 verses. And in the remaining books of the New Testament there are 12 passages totaling 13 verses. Thus we find 126 different passages in the New Testament referring to the resurrection of Christ and our resurrection—totaling 282 verses!

Now let me discuss, first of all after this preliminary matter, the resurrection of our Lord which is passed and the resurrection of believers which, of course, is yet to come. The reasonableness of the hope that Christian believers have for their ultimate resurrection rests firmly on the great historic truth of Christ's own bodily resurrection. This was predicted, then realized, and then interpreted. Over and over again our Lord not only announced that He would rise from the dead, but He actually named the time when He would arise from the dead—on the third day, as in Matthew 12:40; 16:21; 17:23; etc.

There are four great testimonies to the reality of this resurrection which is described in all four Gospels. First, there is the fact of the empty tomb, which was witnessed to by the women, by two of the disciples, and by the angels. Second, there are the ten appearances of our Lord during the forty days between His resurrection on Easter and the Ascension. In the third place, there is the testimony of the angels themselves who said: *He is not here, but is risen.* (Luke 24:3-9). And finally, we have the immediate preaching of the Apostles proclaiming this tremendous fact, even from the day of Pentecost, that Christ had risen from the dead. The first sermon on that great day was a demonstration from the prophetic scriptures, and from the fact of the empty tomb and the appearances of the risen Lord, that God had made this person Jesus, whom the Jews had crucified, both Lord and Christ. The early apostles took seriously the fact that they had been commissioned to be the witnesses of these things, as in Luke 24:46, 47, indeed, all the way through the Book of Acts 3:15; 5:32; 13:31, etc. It was to this fact that Paul constantly alluded in the various defenses he was compelled to make before the rulers of Palestine and Syria. He says: *Of the hope and resurrection of the dead I am called in question,* Acts 23:6; 24:15; 25:19; 26:8, 23. May I say here, before we go on to the next subject of our own resurrection, that I have looked at this theme and written about it now for many, many years—many decades, in fact, and my own opinion is more than ever that the evidence of the resurrection of Christ is incontrovertible. One can deny these records, repudiate them, and say they don't believe in the resurrection, but this evidence is so definite, so basic, so historically grounded, and so tightly put together, that there is just no explanation except that Christ really rose from the dead.

Now I would like to inject something here of a rather startling nature. I was told the last time I was in Palestine that there are two professors in the Hebrew University (in Jerusalem) who themselves acknowledge that probably Jesus Christ did rise from the dead. I would like to look into this a little more in detail, if I should have the privilege of going back to Palestine in the coming days.

Now let's look at the resurrection of believers. Though there are many passages in the New Testament which speak of the resurrection of those who belong to the Lord Jesus when He comes back, the most detailed of all is in the 15th chapter of I Corinthians. I think we do injustice to ourselves by leaving I Corinthians 15 for funerals. I hear it read at all funerals, but rarely have I heard it read from the pulpit. It is a tremendous chapter for you and me, funeral or no funeral.

Paul here sets forth four basic truths regarding the body we shall possess in glory. It will be identical with the earthly body though care must be taken in defining identical. This body will have the qualities of incorruptibility, glory and power. It will be a spiritual body in contrast to our present natural bodies. It will be like unto the body of our Lord Jesus. Don't forget, however, *this is a body*. There will be a similarity between the bodies we now have and those we will have at the resurrection. We will be at home in our resurrection bodies, as we are at home in this body. We will recognize one another. The body that suffered death because of sin will be raised from the dead. Here a mystery arises. Around what will this resurrection be built? Of course the actual corpuscles, the atoms of this fleshly body of ours will not be transformed into a spiritual body. There will exist some kind of a mysterious nucleus around which the resurrection body will be built. If the stalk of wheat must come from a living germ buried in the ground, is there not some hidden germ of our own being around which the Lord Jesus will build our resurrection bodies?

Though our resurrection bodies will not have the identical particles of which the bodies we now indwell are composed, nevertheless they will be raised out of them. How this identity of the two bodies will be maintained the Apostle does not say. It will be a miracle of God. Our resurrection bodies will be as definitely related to the bodies we now have as a stalk of wheat with its kernels is related to the kernels buried in the ground, out of which the stalk came. That is, the kernel dies, but in dying it gives life to that which rises up so that a kernel of wheat does not give birth to barley or oats—it gives birth to the particular kind of wheat it is. On the phrase, sown in dishonour and raised in honour, Dr. Pasche offers some help. "Why does the Apostle say that the body is sown in dishonour? Because the body, good in itself, has become the instrument of sin and our rebellious will. It is with it that we satisfy our lust, that we speak and act as we ought not to. It is therefore important that this body be held firmly in tow to keep it from departing from the right way." Paul says *I buffet my body, I bring it into bondage lest by any means after I have preached to others, I myself should be a castaway.* (Romans 8:13) *If ye through Spirit do mortify the deeds of the body, ye shall live.* Someday this body will be raised in glory. It will no longer have either spot or wrinkle. It will be able to carry out the will of God perfectly. It will be presented as a living sacrifice, holy unto God.

No one fully knows the meaning of the phrase: "A spiritual body." To begin with we should carefully consider Godet's fine definition: "It denotes a body not of the same substance as the soul, otherwise it would not be a body, but formed by the soul and for a soul destined to serve as an organ to that breath of life called in the Bible the psyche, soul, a body formed by and for the principle of life which is altogether spirit. It will be the docile instrument of the spirit, fulfilling the spirit's wishes and thoughts with an inexhaustible power of action. The spirit, the future body's principle of life, is not directly the spirit of God but it is spirit as the higher element of the human personality but acting in its union with the divine Spirit."

Other references to the resurrection of believers are in I Thessalonians 4:16 and I Corinthians 15. The New Testament speaks frequently about our present experience of having risen with Christ, as Romans 6:13; Ephesians 2:6; Colossians 2:12. Both Christ and the Apostles emphasize the fact that we are to be living day by day in that power which was manifested in Christ's resurrection—indeed the relationship of the risen Lord to Christians here on earth in every age is the basic theme of the entire 6th chapter of the Epistle to the Romans.

We come to the end of this chapter with a very sad and tragic subject—the resurrection of the unredeemed. In two places in the New Testament we have references to the resurrection of those who have never received the Lord Jesus Christ. Our Lord says in John 5:29 of those who *shall come forth, they that have done good, unto the resurrection of life; and they that have done evil, unto the resurrection of damnation.* The Apostle Paul says in Acts 24:15, *There will be a resurrection of the dead, both of the just and of the unjust,* referred to in Revelation 20:11-13. While the New Testament says that we will have a body like unto the Lord's own glorious body, there is no hint at all in the scriptures indicating the nature of the resurrection body of unbelievers.

Now I would like to do something at the end of this chapter which I have not done previously. I would like to include an account of a wonderful use of the hope of the resurrection in modern times. This is from the sermon of no less a person than one of the great saints of Europe in the early part of our century, Pastor Martin Niemuller who preached on the resurrection of Christ to a saddened people on Easter morning, March 28, 1937. Let me read from Niemuller's sermon: "Dear Brethren today we feel something of the harshness" (he was in prison at the time) "of that which has been in the world since Easter. The hostility against the preaching of the crucified and risen Saviour has blazed up along the whole world line and on every side people try to persuade us that the old world is really wonderously beautiful—that the old world is on the best road to becoming the new world by its own efforts, and that the message of Jesus Christ is therefore, as far as it deals with the forgiveness of sins, now become superfluous. And a convulsive effort is being made to reclaim Jesus for this side of the old world and to do away with the uniqueness of his life and his death and the mystery of his cross and the resurrection. So they tell us this is a meaningless piece of nonsense. We may well feel frightened with regard to this newly awakened enmity of the whole world. And people do not forget to tell us how few visible guarantees we have for our belief that God will ever create a new world. Is it any wonder that many men and women are beginning to doubt and to lose courage? Does the Easter message of the new world, of the approaching kingdom of God, does this Bible message still hold good, they wonder? Is it not more honest and fitting to make peace with the old world—the pre-Easter world which is after all showing itself to be strong and so powerful? Dear Easter congregation, we can here hold nobody back who wants to go his own way. We live in a time of decisions. It is becoming a time of parting, but it is better for us not to trust what our eyes see. All this will pass away. Our Lord says *Blessed are they that have not seen yet have believed.* Throughout the centuries the risen Christ has gone before his community and today also He goes before us. His victory will be our victory. And just as our fathers in the faith believed in Him, with that assurance which the risen Christ gave to His first disciples, so we too are sure and will continue to proclaim as a believing and professing community that what makes us glad deep down in our hearts in the ups and downs amid which we live in the great world that carries us along with it, I think what makes us glad with the great joy is this, the Lord is risen. He is truly and gloriously risen. Satan, the world, death, sin and hell are quelled forever more, their rage and power brought to naught by Christ whom we endure."

CHAPTER 9

The Signs of the Times

The phrase "signs of the times" does not have a direct religious connotation. The phrase itself occurs only once in the New Testament. And even there (Matthew 16:3) it does not specifically refer to religious matters, and certainly not to the Lord's return.

It is true that our Lord's disciples asked Him (Matthew 24:3) *What shall be the sign of thy coming, and of the end of the world?* But the actual phrase, "the signs of the times," does not occur here in the Olivet Discourse. The word translated *sign* is used for the sign identifying Jesus in the manger (Luke 2:12), and in reference to the experience of Jonah (Luke 11:29), but most frequently it is used in reference to the miracles performed by Christ (Acts 2:22), or by the Apostles (Acts 2:43). However, today and for some centuries, the phrase, "signs of the times," generally is taken to have reference to phenomena indicating the imminent end of this age, or pointing to the imminency of our Lord's return. And this is the way we will use the word now.

First of all, let's consider some notable statements in ages past concerning the signs of the times. From the second century down to this very day students of the scriptures, ecclesiastic authorities, theologians, etc., have held the view that their own generation might witness the end of this age, and that the return of the Lord was near. In the 13th and 14th centuries one of the most widely circulated pieces of literature was what was called *The Fifteen Signs Before Doomsday*. Martin Luther certainly believed that his own generation would terminate with the end of this age. I think that what Luther said is important in his commentary on Luke 21, verses 25-36: "I do not wish to force or constrain anyone to believe as I do; but neither will I permit anyone, on the other hand, to take from me my belief that the day of judgment is not far off." This is four hundred years ago now. "Christ's words and these signs lead me so to believe. For whatever chronicles we may read from the time of Christ until now, we shall not find a parallel to what the world has shown itself within the past century. Such building and planting have never been so common as they are now—so universal, such expensive and varied food and drinks have also never been so usual as in our day. To such an extravagance of expense have people also gone for clothing as to make it impossible to go any futher. And who has ever read of such commercial operations as are now encircling and swallowing up the world? Whilst all descriptions of art and science are coming up and have come the like of which has never been since Christ was born."

Still quoting Luther. "Besides there are people so acute and so knowing as to leave nothing hidden, that is knowledge is advancing so rapidly," (think of this, four hundred years ago) "boys twenty years of age now," says Luther, "know more than doctors used to know. A knowledge of languages, all sorts of wisdom flourishes to a degree compelling us to confess, the world has reached its very culmination in what relates to temporal interests or what Christ called 'the cares of this life'—eating, drinking, building, planning, buying, selling, marrying, doing for children and such like whichsoever considers must acknowledge that it cannot hold much longer. There is a light breaking upon the world and a day coming be it what it may, there has not been in Christendom hitherto such intelligence, such penetration, such mental activity in and about the things of this life to say nothing of the discoveries of printing, firearms and the implements of war." Now Luther catalogued a lot of signs but he was absolutely wrong by thinking he was at the end of the age.

Let us come down to the 19th century. According to that great scholar, Bishop J. C. Ryle, in his work on Luke, written in 1867, he lists the signs of the times, as he believed, for his day as follows: 1. The mission to the heathen. (Luther never mentioned this.) 2. The interest taken in the Jewish nation. 3. The wonderful spread of knowledge and communication between nations. 4. Wars and shaking of nations. 5. The drying up of the Mohammedan power. 6. The increased attention to unfulfilled prophecy.

Now let us take a contemporary of Bishop Ryle, Dr. A. R. Faussett who is one of the three authors of the great *Jamison, Faussett and Brown Bible Commentary,* one of the best biblical scholars of the 19th century and a famous student of prophecy. Faussett's signs of the times around 1880 are the following: The unification of the world. (This is greatly increased since he wrote.) Then, (Luther never mentioned this, neither did Bishop Ryle) lawlessness and worldliness. (Interesting how this unification of the world and lawlessness tremendously increased since Faussett wrote.) Infidelity and waning faith. (Of course by this he meant apostasy.) The preaching of the gospel everywhere. The drying up of the Euphrates River and Mohammedanism. (I want to come back to that, which is very important.) Increase in the study of prophecy. And last, (very important), the restoration of Israel to Palestine.

Before I give a classification of these various phenomena which the scriptures declare will occur at the end of the age, I want to call attention to two of them mentioned by Ryle and Faussett. First, this increasing study of prophecy. In the last quarter of the 19th century there was a great renewed attention given to the study of prophecy. And I think this was also true in the first quarter of our century because of the First World War. I do not believe that there is any great increase in the last twenty-five years in the study of prophecy. I think a great many people know nothing about it, some are interested, but I don't see any movement through the church on this. Some would disagree with me.

The other one is quite significant. The Bishop speaks of, "the drying up of the Mohammedan power." And Faussett speaks of the "drying up of the Euphrates River and Mohammedanism." This is very, very interesting. Many students of prophecy in the 19th century believed that the drying up of the Euphrates River in the Book of Revelation (16:12) was a symbol of the shriveling of Mohammedanism and that this would appear at the end of the age. Now I am sorry to say that Mohammedanism is not shriveling. One thing has passed away—that is, there is no Caliph for Mohammedanism. Up until the First World War there was a head of Mohammedanism in Turkey, but there is none now. The First World War and Kemal Ataturk in Turkey put an end to all of this. But I have never been able to see why the drying up of the Euphrates River should mean the dissolution and reduction of Mohammedanism. Scores of books are written defending this; still I don't see it. I think the drying up of the Euphrates River was to give access to Palestine for the kings of the East coming to the Battle of Armageddon.

Now I would like to classify the phenomena which the scriptures declare will occur at the end of this age. There are six different categories, and two or three that are not included in these categories. Let us see if we can arrange these phenomena under six different headings.

The phenomena in nature would be of a dual nature. First earthquakes (Matthew 24:7; Revelation 6:12, etc.). I have often been asked if I thought that the recent earthquake in Los Angeles had any prophetic significance. Absolutely not, none whatever. When the earthquakes occur which our Lord refers to, and which are frequent in the Book of Revelation, they will be universal and world wide. There will be a great increase of earthquake tremors, but I trust that you and I will not be here. These earthquakes that we have seen in the 20th century are not a fulfillment of these passages. There is another phenomena belonging to *nature*, celestial disturbances as in Matthew 24:29-31; Isaiah 24:23; etc. As soon as the sputniks were pushed into the air, as soon as we began this space exploration, landing on the moon, etc., people began to believe, and some even wrote long articles, that this is the fulfillment of *the stars will fall from heaven, the sun will not give her light,* etc., etc. Don't you believe it. This little bit of hardware that man is shooting up into the sky, that is encircling our globe in various forms, this has nothing to do with the darkening of the moon, or the sun, or violence in the celestial realm. What we have seen now is not a fulfillment of these Biblical prophecies. So these two phenomena in nature, earthquakes and celestial disturbances we observe today should not be interpreted as a sign that we are at the end of the age.

Now second, and rather more important and more specific, there is war and the appearance of specific nations. You have *the northern powers* in Ezekiel 38, you have *the ten kingdoms* of Revelation 17:12; you have *the kings from the east* of Revelation 16:12; you have *a world federation of kings under Antichrist* in Revelation 13:1-8; and the general statements about the increase of wars and rumors of wars. We have never lived in such a militaristic atmosphere as we are living in now. Though it may not be a great war, perhaps by no means the most critical we have ever fought, we have already been ten years in Vietnam. This is the longest war that America has ever fought, and this is on a limited scale. But this mounting up of enormous expenditures in our country, in Great Britain, in Russia, in France, in Germany, in Italy, for war and the implements of war, is a certain sign that we are on the edge of a military convulsion at least. This increase of militarism is very, very important.

Now third, there are moral and ethical phenomena. This I think might be discovered in three different groups of passages. First there is the increase of lawlessness, in Matthew 24:37-39. In the last ten years the world has seen an outburst of rebellion and lawlessness such as modern man has never dreamed. This is exactly what our Lord said. That lawlessness would increase. The word is *iniquity* in the text but that is a weak word—the word is *lawlessness*. Now secondly our Lord said (Matthew 24:37; Luke 17:26), *As in the days of*

Noah, and as in the days of Sodom and Gomorrah.
Let's take the latter. What do we mean by referring to Sodom and Gomorrah? Now I am sorry to use such a plain word that is being used everywhere today. This has to do with homosexuality, of course, and all the various perversions of sexual life. Now, my dear friends, we are not only seeing this today and observing it in our literature and on television, and an actual condoning of it, but we even have churches now for these men who are indulging in this vicious and loathsome vice. This Sodom and Gomorrah situation is, in a strange way, spreading like a heavy mist over the whole civilized world. There is another list in II Timothy, the third chapter, on morality and cruelty. I will leave this with you. So in the decline of ethical standards, in the rebellion against moral virtues such as we are living in today, we are a doomed people indeed, unless we are in Christ.

Fourth, there are ecclesiastical and religious matters, most of all apostasy, as in Luke 18:8, *When the Son of man cometh, shall he find faith on the earth?* See also II Thessalonians 2:10-12; and II Peter 2:17,21; and especially I John 4:1-3. I want to be very careful here as to what I say about apostasy. I believe that there are direful and tragic movements in Christendom today—the denial of the reality of God, the repudiation of the virgin birth and the resurrection—even in so-called religious books. This reduces the historical phenomena and events of the gospel to mere myths, and the false theory that one religion is as good as another and what we need to do is bring all religions together and out of this mixture get one world religion, etc. But I do not believe we are yet in *the* apostasy. We are preparing for it, we are moving in that direction, but I don't think *the* apostasy is yet upon the church.

There is an encouraging and joyous item under this

ecclesiastical and religious phenomena I must introduce here. The apostasy is tragic, but in Matthew 24:14 you have the prediction of the gospel preached to all nations, and this I think is really being fulfilled these days. Think of the enormous outreach of radio in these last thirty years. I read in an article the other day that religious radio broadcasting just celebrated its fiftieth anniversary. That's how young it is. In fact, I was born long before radio broadcasting even began. Then there are gospel recordings, and Christian literature crusades; the enormous crusades of Billy Graham; and the movement of Campus Crusade, etc. So this gospel is being preached throughout the world as it never, never has been before. You have airplanes reaching these mission stations, and all kinds of devices for getting the gospel in their own language including the marvelous work of Wycliffe Translators. So I would think that more people can hear the gospel today, that is by radio, by voice or by reading it, than at any other time in the history of the world.

Now the fifth category has to do with Israel. That Israel will return to her land is frequently stated in the prophets of the Old Testament. That Jerusalem will become a burdensome stone, Zechariah 12:2,3 tells us. That she will experience a great spiritual revival is frequently found in the Old Testament from Isaiah 62 right down to the end of the Old Testament. This return of Israel to Palestine is in my mind one of the greatest phenomena indicating the near approach of our age that we have. I'm not going to dwell on this now; I have written a whole book on this, *Israeli/Arab Conflict*, published by Gospel Light Publications. But I do believe that this return, actually the greatest return of Israel to Palestine since the invasion of Nebuchadnezzar (that would be 2500 years ago), has great significance. I believe this return of two million Jews from

105 different nations back to their homeland, speaking Hebrew and studying Hebrew, and obeying the sabbath day, I think this phenomena is probably in some ways the most significant setting of the stage for the end of the age that we have.

Now one more subject concerning the appearance of certain individuals. The return of Elijah in Malachi 4: the two witnesses in Jerusalem, Revelation 11; the false Christs and false prophets in the Olivet Discourse and Antichrist of I John 4:3 and Revelation 13:1-10. Of all of these which do you think are the most significant and the most clearly revealed as to fulfilling prophecy today? I would say they are these: militarism, lawlessness, deepening unbelief, the world-wide preaching of the gospel and the return of Israel to Palestine.

There is another one in Matthew 24:30, *the sign of the Son of man in heaven.* Actually no one dogmatically knows what this sign is. There have been various interpretations—I am not even suggesting one here.

In the last two hundred years many books have been written about the Roman Catholic Church in prophecy, especially in relation to Revelation 17. I have my own conviction about this: that attempts to discover history of major events in Europe and the Roman Catholic Church in the Book of Revelation have again and again proved confusing and inaccurate. Of course, all schemes for ascertaining the year of Christ's return by juggling chronological data in the Bible are doomed to failure. Now we might do well to conclude this brief summary with the well-chosen words of one of the great students of prophecy here in America in the latter part of the 19th century, George Peters.

"The signs preceding the first stage of the advent are all of such nature that appear more or less in every generation. And hence in view of their continued existence have caused men in the various succeeding centuries to hold, as Gregory the Great, Martin Luther and others, that the end was very near because the signs indicative of the end were really present. Many of them were painfully present, and it is to the honor and piety of these believers in the Word that they recognized them and assumed the posture of servants looking for the coming of the Master. It is reasonable to suppose that signs will assume a greater magnitude" (this is very important) as the time of the end draws nigh." Let me interrupt here just a moment on this. As some of you know, there were a number of books written in the early part of the 19th century declaring that Napoleon was Antichrist. And then a little bit later there were a lot more books written that Napoleon III was Antichrist, and both Napoleon the Conqueror and Napoleon III did have some characteristics of Antichrist. A student of prophecy one time said to me that he wouldn't be a bit surprised if Satan *thought* that Napoleon would be Antichrist, but when God was through with Napoleon He took him off the stage. The time had not come in God's program for the Antichrist to appear. Now I go back to Peter's sentence: "It is reasonable to suppose that such signs will assume a greater magnitude as the time of the end draws nigh. Or at least that they will appear in such proportions that the believing for whom alone they are intended can not mistake in their presence and in their import that they are in the end of the age."

CHAPTER 10

Final Destiny

It is a strange paradox that while the great systematic theologies of the 19th century, such as those by Strong, Shedd, Hodge, etc. gave far more attention to the subject of hell than to the subject of heaven, yet in the teaching and preaching ministry of the church, the situation has been the very reverse. Almost all congregations have heard, some frequently, messages of heaven; but in so many of our churches, even Evangelical churches, no message is heard from year to year, and sometimes from decade to decade, on what the Bible says about the final destiny of the unsaved. And the ignoring of this is not rightly dividing the word of truth, when the New Testament has so much to say about this very, very solemn theme.

Let us look first of all at general terms, then the locality of hell, the eternity of hell, and other characteristics. In the New Testament there is a frequently occurring word for those who die without Christ which is "perish" or to be "lost," translated from the Greek word *Apollumi*. This is the word used when referring to bottles that are broken (Matthew 9:17), or a coin or a sheep that is lost (Luke 15). It is used with reference to men about to die (Luke 8:24), and of the prodigal son (Luke 15:24). This is the word often used by St. Paul of those who go out into eternity unsaved, as in I Corinthians 1:18; 15:18; II Thessalonians 2:10 as well as in the two seldom considered words of our Lord who can destroy both soul and body in hell (Matthew 10:28).

The noun form of this important word lost or perish is "destruction" or "perdition." Judas is called the son of perdition (John 17:12). Jesus used this word in that famous statement regarding the broad way that leadeth to destruction (Matthew 7:13). And the enemies of the cross, we are told in Philippians 3:19, have their end as destruction. Twice this idea of destruction is referred to in relation to the destiny of the unsaved when it is a translation of another word (II Thessalonians 1:9).

We must take the actual word for the condition or the place or the locality of the lost in eternity. We were just looking now at the general term "perish" or to be "lost." *Sheol* is a word appearing 65 times in the Hebrew Old Testament. In other words, it is a Hebrew word. In the King James version, the Hebrew *Sheol* is translated "grave" 31 times, "hell" 31 times, and "the pit" 3 times. But in the *American Revised Version* the word uniformly is not translated at all, just left as *Sheol*. It was invariably translated "Hades" in the Greek Old Testament of which we will have more to say in a moment. This word then, generally speaking, was the place to which the spirits of the dead descended. Important passages are Psalm 16:10 and Ezekiel 32:23.

"Hades" occurs 11 times in the New Testament. It is an ancient Greek word, appearing scores of times at the dawn of Greek literature in Homer, and means basically the abode of the dead. In Greek literature it has nothing to do with religion, just the abode of the dead. The rich man of Luke 16:23 was in Hades. Acts 2:27, 31 is a quotation from Psalm 16:10. It is personified in I Corinthians 15:55. Hades is never used in the New Testament as the equivalent for hell.

The third word is "hell." Hell in our New Testament is the translation of an Aramaic word *Gehenna* derived from the Hebrew word *Gehinnom*, that is the Valley of *Hinnom*. The Valley of Hinnom was a place south of Jerusalem where fires were continually burning for the destruction of garbage. Later, tragically, children were wickedly offered there as sacrifices (Joshua 15:8; 18:16; II Chronicles 28:3 and especially Isaiah 66:24).

This word "hell" as a translation of *Gehenna* occurs 12 times in the New Testament. Always, with the single exception of James 3:6, it occurs as an utterance of Jesus (Matthew 5:22,29,30; 10:28; 18:9; 23:15,33 and Luke 12:5). I have heard many people who are not believers often say in a glib way. "The Sermon on the Mount is good enough for me." But never forget that in the Sermon on the Mount Jesus uses the word "hell" more often than in any other discourse that He ever uttered. And if the Sermon on the Mount is good enough for them, they should put a little weight on the meaning of these tragic verses.

In II Peter 2:4 in The King James Version, "hell" is a translation of the Greek word *Tartarus* and generally refers to the place of fallen angels.

Then in Revelation 9:1 and 9:11 you have the phrase, "the bottomless pit," which is the word "Abyss" out of which the beast arises in Revelation 11:7; 17:8. It is in this place, the abyss, that Satan is chained for a thousand years (Revelation 20:1,3). Now let's look again at these words because we want to take one more.

Sheol, Old Testament word, *Hades,* place of the departed spirits, *hell, Tartarus,* the *bottomless pit* and finally, we find *hell* described as "the lake of fire and brimstone." Jesus often referred to this fire, but it is especially emphasized toward the end of the Book of Revelation. Revelation 19:20, chapter 20—this is where people are consigned to hell, chapter 20, verses 10,14,15, and chapter 21, verse 8.

Now with these various words for hell, let us take up the tragic subject that the final state of the wicked is one of punishment. The eternal fate of those who have refused Christ is the result of the wrath of God. This wrath of God you will find designated sometimes as the day of wrath (Romans 2:5,8; 9:22; I Thessalonians 5:9; Colossians 3:6). However, it is, even as we might expect, that God's wrath is most often referred to in the Book of Revelation, as in 6:16 and 17; 11:18; 14:10 and especially 16:19. The wrath of God is sometimes expressed by the Greek word *thumos* which is sometimes used of Satan's wrath as in Revelation 12:12 or *the wrath of Babylon,* Revelation 14:8, but most of all *the wrath of God,* 16:1,19. Hell is a place of punishment. Two Greek words expressing punishment occur in two New Testament passages. One in our Lord's great prophetic message Matthew 25:46: *These shall go away into everlasting punishment.* Then in Hebrews 10:29 where the word is *timoria.* Trench says that this word expresses the idea, "punishment as satisfying the inflictor's sense of outraged justice, defending his own honor and the honor of violated law."

We must consider some characteristics of hell. It is

often referred to as a place of darkness, as in Matthew 8:12; 22:13. This has no doubt some bearing on the three hours of darkness at the time of our Lord's crucifixion (Matthew 27:45). Really, darkness is the state of believers even in this life as in John 3:19; Romans 2:19, etc. In darkness you can't see. You don't even know if someone is near you. You don't even know where you are going. This is a time of fear: an environment of hopelessness. Moreover the New Testament says it is a time of suffering. This is referred to by our Lord, in Matthew 8:12, and in the revelation of the state of Dives and Lazarus, where Dives says to Abraham, "I am in torment." This is not yet hell, only hades (Luke 16:23,28). Sometimes it is not only referred to as darkness, and a place of suffering, but as "the second death," in Revelation 2:11 and 20:14, which is also a continuation of the state of the unsaved who are now out of Christ, dead in trespasses and sins. The conception of suffering as expressed by fire is frequently found on the lips of our Lord (Matthew 5:22; 18:8,9; II Peter 3:7) especially Jude 7, "The vengeance of eternal fire."

I have heard many, many people ask, "How can there be the torment of fire in hell when the unredeemed do not have bodies." Who said they do not have bodies? There is a resurrection of the just and the unjust. The unsaved will have some kind of a body. I wouldn't argue about this word fire; whatever it is, it's fire. I don't think we need to get dogmatic here at all. It is a place of great suffering, expressed by our Lord himself as fire.

Now a very important theme regarding hell. The punishment of the unredeemed is *eternal.* Many argue about this, and many cults have been founded to repudiate this, but all we need here are the scriptures.

The word used to indicate the endlessness of such

punishment is the Greek word *Aioonios*. It is used in the following passages in relation to eternal punishment (Matthew 18:8; II Thessalonians 1:9; Hebrews 6:2, etc.). Now notice, this word *Aioonios*, used to express the time of punishment of the unredeemed, is the same word used of the eternity of God or the eternity of the Trinity—and particularly the eternity of the Holy Spirit (Romans 16:26; I Timothy 6:16; Revelation 1:18; John 14:17). If it relates to the eternity of God, it must also relate to the eternity of this matter of punishment. It is used over and over again in reference to the eternal blessedness of the saints (Matthew 19:16,29; John 6:54; Luke 18:30 and especially Matthew 25:46). The word *Aioonios* occurs 66 times in the Greek New Testament. Of these, 51 refer to the happiness of the righteous! That is, if their happiness is eternal, the punishment is eternal too. Of these, 51 out of 66 refer to the happiness of the righteous, 7 to the duration of God as eternal, 7 in perpetuity of the future punishment of the wicked.

I would like to conclude with a passage from Dr. Charles Hodge's great *Systematic Theology*. Every word here is important. "The common doctrine is" (that is in the church) "that the conscious existence of the soul after the death of the body is unending." I repeat, "The common doctrine is that the conscious existence of the soul after the death of the body is unending." That there is no repentance or reformation. That those who depart this life unreconciled to God remain forever in this state of alienation and are forever sinful and miserable. This is the doctrine of the whole church. "It is obvious that this is a question that can be decided only by divine relation. No one can reasonably assume to decide how long the wicked are to suffer for their sins upon any general principle of right and wrong. The conditions of the problem are not within our grasp. If we can believe the Bible to be the Word of God, all we have to do is to ascertain what it teaches on this subject and humbly submit to that teaching. "It is a doctrine that the natural heart revolts from and struggles against and to which it submits only under stress of authority. The Church believes the doctrine because it must believe it or renounce faith in the Bible and give up the hopes that are founded on its premises."

May I end with a statement by the French theologian Rene Pasche in his book, *The Future Life*. "If all men and women will necessarily come to salvation, let us leave them alone and everything will come out just fine, but if eternal hell really threatens them then let us not give ourselves any rest but imitate our Lord who knowing the abyss about to swallow us up, came down to snatch us from it."

CHAPTER 11

The Millennium

In the basic themes of Biblical Eschatology, the Church down through the ages has been quite agreed; that is the Church Universal has believed in the second advent of Christ, in the resurrection from the dead, in the day of judgment, in heaven and in hell. Basically the entire Christian Church, whatever their variations in detail, have agreed on these great themes.

But there are three subjects in the realm of Biblical Eschatology in which there has been a great deal of difference. One of them is in the Book of Revelation, for which four different principles of interpretation have been proposed, and when you follow one line of interpretation you are wholly disagreeing with the other three. There are tremendous differences in the meaning and symbolism of the Book of Revelation. Second, the Christian Church has always been divided in regard to Israel. A large part of the church does not believe there is any future for the State of Israel, or that prophecy has anything to do with Palestine at the end of this age. This is a large segment of the Church, including Luther and Calvin. And then third, there is the vast difference in approaching the subject of the millennium. In fact, there are what we call a-millenialists, post-millennialists, and pre-millennialists. Concerning these three we will have something to say later in our study.

The word "millennium" in itself does not have a religious connotation such as, second advent, resurrection, judgment, etc. Millennium is a combination of two Latin words, *Mille* meaning thousand and *Annum*, from which we get annual, meaning a year. We use this Latin word *Mille* occasionally in its original connotation as the mills in currency, in one-tenth of a cent and one-thousandth of a dollar. This also enters into our word million, that is, a thousand times a thousand. From *annum* comes anniversary, etc. In fact millennium can express a desire for a condition of blessedness, apart from religious factors. One recent dictionary gives this as a definition of millennium: "A period of prevailing future or great happiness or perfect government. A freedom from familiar ills and imperfections of human existence." So like a great many words of the New Testament and the Christian Faith, this word millennium really belongs in the New Testament for its theme is enlarged in a way and becomes a common term for all those things we expect to occur at the end of this age.

Now the only place in the Bible where there is predicted a time limit for this great period to come when Christ will be reigning on earth is the opening paragraph of the 20th chapter of the Book of Revelation, where the phrase *the thousand years* appears six times in this opening paragraph! *I saw an angel come down from heaven, having the key of the bottomless pit and a great chain in his hand. And he laid hold on the dragon, that old serpent, which is the Devil, and Satan, and bound him a thousand years, and cast him into the bottomless pit, and shut him up, and set a seal upon him, that he should deceive the nations no more, till the thousand years should be fulfilled: and after that he must be loosed a little season.*

I hope you will not be offended if I introduce an anecdote of many, many years ago here regarding the shutting up of Satan. Around 1910, before the First World War, our world seemed to be filled with sunshine, peace and the hope that perhaps we were on the verge of universal peace, really on the verge of the millennium. That was a wonderful time that will never be restored until the Lord comes back. Somebody said to the great Baptist preacher Dr. Riley, "I wouldn't be a bit surprised if we are in the millennium." He replied, "Well, I doubt it. In my Bible it says that during the millennium Satan will be chained and shut up for a thousand years. If this is the millennium, all I would say is that Satan has a long chain."

Now I go to verse 4, *I saw thrones, and they sat upon them, and judgment was given unto them: and I saw the souls of them that were beheaded for the witness of Jesus, and for the word of God, and which had not worshipped the beast, neither his image, neither had received his mark upon their foreheads, or in their hands; and they lived and reigned with Christ a thousand years. But the rest of the dead lived not again until the thousand years were finished. This is the first resurrection. Blessed and holy is he that hath part in the first resurrection: on such the second death hath no power, but they shall be priests of God and of Christ, and shall reign with him a thousand years.*

One should carefully note where this paragraph is located in the scriptures chronologically. It is *after* the Battle of Armageddon when the marshalled hosts of Christ's enemies are defeated and the Beast and the False Prophet have been consigned to the lake of fire. This paragraph opens with two references to the chaining of Satan during the thousand year period. And then we have two references to the saints of Christ reigning with him a thousand years.

The late Professor Charles in his famous work on the Book of Revelation, and he is not normally an advocate of the principles which we have been studying together, frankly acknowledges, "the prophecy of the millennium in chapter 20 must be taken literally as it was by the early church fathers who unanimously believed in a millennium to come. The very fact that in verse 16, chapter 19 the Christ who appears at the Battle of Armageddon has for one of his names King of kings implies that the millennium which this event introduces will have much to do with the government or the rule of Christ."

Now we must go back into the Old Testament to obtain some light on the conditions of the millennium. The kingly aspect of the person and the work of Christ, can be traced back to the great promise made to David, the founder of the Messianic line, through whom, as King of Israel, Christ derives His right to the Davidic throne. In II Samuel 7:13,16 we read: *I will establish the throne of his kingdom forever . . . Thy throne shall be established forever.* This great initial promise to David is referred to again and again in the Old Testament historical books, as in I Kings 2:45; 8:25; 9:5; I Chronicles 22:10 and Psalms 21; 89; 132.

The passage in II Samuel 7:16 is the promise which the angel quoted at the time of the annunciation to the Virgin Mary, that He, who was to be born of her, was to sit on the throne of His father, David (Luke 1:32,33).

Now let's remember something about the throne of the father, David. This is not in heaven. *This is on earth.* David had no throne in heaven, and David's Son as such, will not have a throne in heaven. His throne is on the earth—that is as the Son of David.

Probably the greatest single passage in the Old Testament regarding the benedictions and blessings of the millennial kingdom yet to come, and certainly there is no kingdom on earth today that is the kingdom of Christ, would be the 11th chapter of Isaiah. This is one of the greatest chapters in the whole of the Word of God. *There shall come forth a rod out of the stem of Jesse* (now you remember Jesse was the father of David, so this has to do in a round about way with David, David's seed, and David's throne), *and a Branch shall grow out of his roots: And the spirit of the Lord shall rest upon him, the spirit of wisdom and understanding, the spirit of counsel and might, the spirit of knowledge and of the fear of the Lord. . . . But with righteousness shall he judge the poor, and reprove with equity for the meek of the earth: and he shall smite the earth with the rod of his mouth, and with the breath of his lips shall he slay the wicked. And righteousness shall be the girdle of his loins, and faithfulness the girdle of his reins. The wolf also shall dwell with the lamb, and the leopard shall lie down with the kid; and the calf and the young lion and the fatling together; and a little child shall lead them . . . They shall not hurt nor destroy in all my holy mountain; for the earth shall be full of the knowledge of the Lord, as the waters cover the sea. And in that day there shall be a root of Jesse, which shall stand for an ensign of the people; to it shall the Gentiles seek: and his rest shall be glorious.* In other words a kingdom of God is to be established on this earth.

This is one of the great themes of Old Testament

prophecy. This is what the Book of Revelation refers to about our reigning with Christ; this is on earth—the millennium is an earthly theme not a heavenly theme. It is to this millennial reign that Daniel so often refers, as in Daniel 2:44 and 7:27. May I note once again, the prominence of the reign of righteousness. We saw it in the passage from Isaiah, and let me quote another which we seldom look at in the New Testament: I Corinthians 15. We always say that this is a chapter on the resurrection. But in the middle of this chapter, beginning with verse 23, going down to verse 28, is one of the most remarkable passages on the kingdom of Christ and the reign of Christ that we have in the New Testament. Notice the conflict here and the overwhelming victory over the enemies of God. I begin with verse 23: *Every man in his own order: Christ the firstfruits; afterward they that are Christ's at his coming. Then cometh the end, when he shall have delivered up the kingdom to God,* (this is the end of the kingdom; we will come back to the first in a minute) *even the Father; when he shall have put down all rule and all authority and power. For he must reign, till he hath put all enemies under his feet.* Now beloved, where are these enemies? Why, they are on earth. They are not in heaven. *The last enemy that shall be destroyed is death. For he hath put all things under his feet.* You mean already? *But when he saith all things are put under him, it is manifest that he is excepted, which did put all things under him.* This is future now. *. . . then shall the son also himself be subject unto him that put all things under him, that God may be all in all.* I want to repeat verse 24: *Then cometh the end, when he shall have delivered up the kingdom to God, . . . when he shall have put down all rule and all authority and power.* He shall be King of kings and Lord of lords—He will be ruling the nations of the earth, in the Old and New Testament both. And how we need it today!

Now let us look for a moment at some characteristics of the millennium. First, this will be a time of universal, undisturbed peace. Let me read here Isaiah 2:4, *He shall judge among the nations.* I want to ask you something, do you think the Lord is judging between the nations today? Do you think the Lord is ruling the rulers of the earth today? Not at all. They are rebelling against Him. Now notice this promise. *He shall judge among the nations...* (that is a famous line) *Shall rebuke many people; and they shall beat their swords into plowshares, and their spears into pruning hooks;* (This is a great promise.) *nations shall not lift up sword against nation neither shall they learn war anymore.*

I am sure that there are millions of people on earth today who rejoice in such a longing as this. I mean millions of people outside of the church. I am sure that millions of people in Southeast Asia would be glad to welcome such a time as this *when they shall beat their swords into plowshares and their spears into pruning hooks and nation will not lift up sword against nation.* There are millions of people who would love to see a prophecy like this in its fulfillment. But this is not what man is going to bring about. This is what the Lord Jesus will accomplish. The kings of the earth will not usher in a reign of peace; it will be the Prince of Peace who subdues these warring nations who will then begin this millennium of peace.

The second characteristic is that it will be a universal time of prosperity and abundance. One cannot go into Egypt today and go up the Valley of the Nile, or in the Delta, and see these hundreds of thousands and millions of people living in mud huts, eking out a bare existence—thin and emaciated, without realizing that many people on this earth go to bed hungry from the time they are born until they die. Think of the millions of hungry people in India today. I have not been to India, but many of my friends have, and they say they never want to go back again. The sights of the starving people on the streets of Calcutta and the other great cities of India are just overwhelming in the misery they reveal. The millennium will be a time of unusual prosperity when there will be abundance for everyone. Isaiah 30:15-33; Isaiah 40;49,51,52.

Third, the reign of Christ on earth will be marked by absolute, righteous judgment, meted out to the poor and the rich. Recently I noticed on television that certain people in our country were trying to get justice in certain offices in a large city. Their complaint was that they complained and complained and came down and interviewed one officer after another officer and did everything within their power to get compensation to which they were due. And yet they said the same thing happened day after day and month after month with no results. And many a man today has had a raw deal in the courts and many who are guilty have had very liberal treatment in many of our courts. I repeat, in the millennium the reign of Christ on earth (what a wonderful day) will be marked by absolute, righteous judgment, meted out to the poor and to the rich alike.

Fourth, there will be a wonderful restoration on this earth of the phenomena of nature returning to its original glory and beneficent influence. Violence, cyclones, earthquakes, poisonous plants, choking weeds and burning deserts will disappear. Isaiah writes of this in the 11th chapter and also in chapter 35:1-9; 43:18,19; 55:13; 65:21.

Fifth, and this does not exhaust the theme, during this time Israel will return to Palestine and to the Lord and will enjoy the great blessedness promised to her by the prophets of old, Jeremiah 32:37; Hosea 3:4,5, etc.

I remember once years ago, before Israel was established in Palestine, that two other men and I were standing on a prominent street in Jerusalem, the old Arab Jerusalem. We had been there some years before, and we became a little bewildered by all the new buildings that had been erected. A young woman came by to speak to us, a Jewish woman. She was a teacher in Columbia University. We remarked to her, "What are you over here for?" And she said, "God only knows, I had to come. My people are in trouble." Even then the Jews were being killed. So I said to her "Someday the Messiah will come and all of this will be blotted out." And she said almost in a cry, "Oh," she said, "would that He would come today." This is what will happen to Israel when the Lord returns.

In the phrase, Matthew 19:28, *In the regeneration when the Son of man shall sit on the throne of his glory* is a reference to this millennial reign from the lips of our Lord. Acts 3:19 is another one, *The times refreshing shall come from the presence of the Lord.* And then in the sermon of Simon Peter (Acts 3:21), *The time of restitution of all things, which God hath spoken by the mouth of all his holy prophets since the world began.*

May I call your attention to these three words, even though we considered them previously, in Matthew 19:28—*the regeneration;* in Acts 3:19, *the times of refreshing;* Acts 3:21, *the times of restitution.* These are wonderful Greek words. Finally, there is the prediction in Romans 8:21 that the day would come when the creation itself shall be delivered from the bondage of corruption into the glorious liberty of the children of God.

It is true that there will be a great rebellion of a vast multitude at the end of the millennium—indicating that not everyone will be submissive to the reign of

Christ. It has been rightly said that the millennium does not call for the removal of all satanic influences and temptations from the life of mankind either in its individual or social aspects, though no doubt Christ's rule with a rod of iron will powerfully hold them in check.

There is one matter we must consider here and that's the three-fold view of the millennium. There are some called the a-millennialists who do not believe in the millennium at all. They interpret this passage in the Book of Revelation, chapter 20, as merely a spiritual symbol that refers to the ultimate reign of Christ in the universe forever. But that is not what the passage says. There is a limit here of the thousand years. Incidentally, some, including great scholars, truly great scholars, such as Warfield of Princeton, make the tragic mistake, and one can hardly know how they could do it, insisting that the millennium was a thousand year period but that it began with Constantine—back in the early centuries. Now, beloved, the time from Constantine on for a thousand years in your text book and my text book in college was called the dark ages, the middle ages. That was no millennium.

The a-millennialists believe there will be no millennium. But there must be a time for Christ to reign on the throne of David on this earth. This is the summing up of the Davidic kingdom on which the Old Testament and the New Testament have so much to say.

In the old days there was the viewpoint, called postmillennialism, that there will be a millennium, but at the end of the millennium, the Lord will return. Now what is meant by this? That the world would get better and better and better. That more and more millions every year would accept the Gospel. That peace would be quite universal—that there would be a time of righteousness and obedience to the law. That the church, like leaven, would penetrate the whole world, and then when everything was wonderful, and beautiful, lovely and sweet, the millennium would be brought about by the Church and Christians, at the end of which Christ would come. This is post-millennialism—the church introduces the millennium or Christ's return terminates the millennium. You don't hear much of this today for one reason. The world is in a much worse condition now than it has ever been. Two world wars, in one-half of a century, and millions of Christians in Japan and China and northern Korea and parts of Africa murdered because they were loyal to the Lord Jesus. Beloved, at least we must acknowledge this, that the Church does not seem to be successful in bringing about a millennial condition. Naturally many people have given up this post-millennialism.

The true view is known as pre-millenialism, that is, the Lord will return before the millennium. All these wonderful characteristics we have been describing—this universal peace, this reign of righteousness, this time of prosperity and joy and loveliness and obedience to the law—all of this will be created not by the Church, not by people now living on earth, but will be introduced by the coming of the omnipotent and powerful Son of God, the King of kings and Lord of lords. So by the very circumstances of this century we are inclined surely to a pre-millennial view.

Pre-millennialists then are those who believe that the millennium will be introduced when the Lord returns. It is very interesting that in the original *Reference Scofield Bible,* in the first edition in 1909 and in the revision of 1917, there is no reference to the millennium and there is no note for Revelation 20. In the new *Scofield Bible* there is a paragraph which makes amends for this.

CHAPTER 12

Our Eternal Home

Of the hundreds of occurrences of the word heaven in the English Bible, almost all of them are translations of the Hebrew word *Shamayim* and the Greek word *Ouranos*. The Hebrew word means literally, "The Heights," while the Greek word has a related but slightly different meaning "That which is raised up."

Considering all the various shades of meaning which may be said to attach to the original words, and to the English word, it is undeniable that the primary meaning of the actual word heaven is, "That which is above." By this is meant, of course, that which is above man or above the earth. As an adverb, heavenly, or as an adjective, it may mean: radiant, spiritual, pure in heart, unearthly, angelic. Some of these ideas are found in the definition of the word "heavenly" in the *Oxford*

English Dictionary: "Having the excellence, beauty, delight that belongs to heaven. Of more than earthly or human excellence, divine." So to be "heavenly-minded" says the *Oxford English Dictionary* is "Having the thoughts and affections set on things above. Holy and devout." They are almost quoting the New Testament. Before we look into the matter of heaven as our home, we should have it clearly in mind that there are three different heavens in the Bible.

First of all, the atmospheric heavens, i.e. the atmosphere that surrounds the earth which we breathe, contained in the sphere known as the troposphere, which does not extend more than 12 miles above the earth. All normal clouds are within 7 miles from the earth. The region beyond the troposphere is known as the stratosphere, and the space above that, 30 to 50 miles is the mesosphere. An interesting phrase is in Deuteronomy 11:11. *The rain of heaven.* Or Psalm 147:8 *Who covereth the heavens with clouds.* We often read of the birds of heaven. Now this is the atmospheric heaven surrounding the earth which you and I live in. Then there are the celestial heavens, the sphere in which the sun, the moon and the stars appear. It is repeatedly stated that they are in the heavens. Even at the very beginning of the record of creation we have the phrase, *Lights in the firmament of the heaven,* Genesis 1:15. The stars are said to be in heaven. Over and over again we read, as the writer of the Hebrews reminds us in Hebrews 1:10, *The heavens are the works of thine hands.* That is the *celestial* heaven.

When we read in the song of Deborah and Barak that after the defeat of Sisera "they fought from heaven; the stars in their courses fought against Sisera" (Judges 5:20), we must of course take this as a poetic way of expressing the fact that even the elements of nature participated in the defeat of this pagan king.

Even though we are told in the scriptures (I Kings 8:27) that the heaven of heavens cannot contain God, and that God is everywhere present on the earth and in heaven (Deuteronomy 4:39), nevertheless the same scriptures clearly state that God does dwell particularly in heaven, designated in the scriptures as *His habitation*. God is often referred to as the God of heaven, especially by Gentile rulers as in Daniel 2:18,19. Of course all Christians are familiar with the great phrase of Matthew 6:9, *Our father which art in heaven*.

There are six English words which are used in the Old and New Testament in reference to heaven in all of which is the idea of dwelling or habitation. It is profoundly significant that all these six terms are used first of all in reference to the tabernacle where God dwelt among His people Israel. Without going into detail they are as follows: Tabernacle, Revelation 13:6; Sanctuary, Hebrews 8:2 and 9:8; Habitation, II Chronicles 30:27; The House, as *In my Father's house are many mansions*, John 14:2; Temple, II Samuel 22:7; and The Throne of God, Isaiah 66.1. Let me go over these words again: Tabernacle, Sanctuary, Habitation, House, Temple, Throne of God.

All of these terms have one common denominator, or one basic characteristic often specifically expressed, that is, Holiness. Thus the Holy Tabernacle and the Holy Place, the Holy of Holies and later the Holy Temple, find their fundamental characteristic, Holiness, eternally perfected in what is called in the scriptures, The Holy City. Only those who have been made holy by the grace of God will dwell in it.

Heaven is so vitally and so commonly referred to as the abode of God in the scriptures that, actually, it is used in both the Old and the New Testament as a synonym for God. Generally the phrase looking up to heaven implies that one looks in that direction, because there is where God abides to whom he will be praying, as in the prayer our Lord taught His disciples to pray, Matthew 14:19. Or in the experience of St. Stephen who looked up into the heavens and saw the Lord, Acts 7:55.

It is quite plain that when Jehovah said unto Moses (Exodus 9:22) *Stretch forth thine hand toward heaven, that there may be hail in all the land of Egypt,* the implication is not that he simply lifted up his hand as a token of authority, but that he appealed to God by lifting up his hand to heaven. This idea of heaven as a synonym for God is fully understood in the confession of the Prodigal Son, (Luke 15:18), *I have sinned against heaven,* that is, against God.

Now before we come to the subject of heaven as our home, in which believers are most interested, we should remind ourselves of the glorious relationship of Jesus Christ Himself to heaven. This is fourfold.

First, in his incarnation *He came down from heaven,* (John 3:13). That is why He refers to Himself as *the manna coming down from heaven,* John 6:33-51. In His incarnation He came down from heaven. This is not true of anyone else who has ever lived on this earth.

Second, He ascended into heaven, as in John 16:28 and especially Luke 24:51; Acts 1:11 and I Timothy 3:16. *He ascended into heaven and sitteth on the right hand of God the Father Almighty.* First He came from heaven, second He ascended into heaven.

Third, He is now engaged in His intercessory work in heaven as our great High Priest. This is especially set forth in Hebrews 8, 9 and 10, where are some of the most amazing passages to be found in the Word of God as to the high priesthood of our Lord.

Fourth, He will return from heaven as in Acts 3:21 and I Thessalonians 4:16: *The Lord himself shall de-*

scend from heaven with a shout, with the voice of the archangel, referred to also in II Thessalonians 1:7,8.

To sum up: in the incarnation He came down from heaven. After the incarnation He ascended into heaven. His present intercessory work is in heaven; and finally He will return from Heaven.

What we want to consider now is the relation of the believer to heaven, as in the promise of the heavenly reward in Matthew 5:10-12 and many such passages as Luke 12:21; Ephesians 1:14 and I Peter 1:3-5.

Everyone is interested in the occupations of believers in heaven, but we do not have too much information in the New Testament about what we will be doing when we are in heaven with the Lord. At least five great facts are set forth regarding the redeemed in Glory. There is that pregnant sentence, *his servants shall serve him* (Revelation 22:3). This is one of the most significant of all. The word translated "servant" is the one so frequently used by St. Paul referring to the present relationship of believers to the Lord Jesus. *We are his servants now* (Ephesians 6:6), and by the other apostles, II Peter 1:1 and James 1:1. The word is found with almost unexpected frequency in the Book of Revelation, 1:1; 7:3; 10:7; 11:18.

These concepts of service and regard for faithfulness are basic themes in our Lord's teaching concerning His return. Thus we may safely say, as many have, that there will be a number of activities in heaven which will be a continuation of our labor for Christ on earth without exhaustion or weariness or failure.

Now another theme that we have in the New Testament regarding our activity in heaven is that of worship. May I refer here to Revelation 19, the opening verses, *I heard a great voice of much people in heaven, saying, Alleluia; Salvation, and glory, and honour, and power, unto our Lord our God: For true and righteous*

*are his judgments . . . and again they said, Alleluia
. . . And the four and twenty elders and the four (living
creatures) fell down and worshipped God . . . And I
heard as it were the voice of a great multitude, and as
the voice of many waters, and as the voice of mighty
thunderings, saying, Alleluia . . . for the Lord God omnipotent reigneth. Let us be glad and rejoice, and give
honour to him: for the marriage of the Lamb is come,
and his wife* (you and me—the church) *hath made herself ready. And to her was granted that she should be
arrayed in fine linen . . .*

And there is the continuation of worship which we do not too often dwell on, while we are here in this flesh.

Then there is the matter of authority. In two of His parables our Lord speaks of assigning authority to faithful servants upon His return. In the parable of the pounds which were distributed to His servants, to two of them He gave *authority over ten cities and over five cities,* Luke 19:17,19. In the parable of the talents, He says to the good and faithful servants: *I will set thee over many things, enter thou into the joy of the Lord.*

We must acknowledge that we really do not know specifically how the servants of the Lord will exercise this authority Christ speaks of, but apparently it refers to activity here on earth, during and after the millennium. I would at this point like to introduce an idea which I have not seen in any volume. In my own book on *The Biblical Doctrine of Heaven* (page 193), "May there not be here some relationship to the idea of what the Apostle calls, the inheritance of the Christian? Ephesians 1:11,14; Colossians 3:24."

Now I realize that this inheritance is first of all something spiritual, immaterial, involving eternal life and righteousness, but is there not something more here than inheriting eternal life? The Apostle Paul in Romans

4:13, speaks of the promises made to Abraham which involved the fact that he, Abraham, should be the heir of the world. Now this is certainly not basically something spiritual. In the same Epistle, 8:17, the Apostle says we should be the heirs of God and joint heirs with Christ. Certainly Christ was never an heir of eternal life. These things He possessed from eternity. The inheritance here spoken of in relation to Christ is somewhat like Psalm 2:8, *Ask of me, and I will give thee the heathen for thine inheritance, and the uttermost parts of the earth for thy possession.*

There is service, worship, authority—and then this glorious matter of fellowship. I would like to refer to a work, two centuries old, by Archbishop Whately on the matter of friendship in heaven. "I am convinced that the extension and perfection of friendship constitute a great part of the future happiness of the blessed. Many have lived in various and distant ages and countries who have been, in their characters, in the agreement of their tastes, the suitableness of dispositions, perfectly adapted for friendship with each other, but who of course could never meet in this world. Many a one, when he is reading history, selects some one or two favorite characters with whom he feels that a personal acquaintance would be peculiarly delightful to him. Why should not such a desire be realized in the future state? A wish to see and know, for example, the Apostle Paul or John is the most likely to arise in the noblest and the purest mind. I would be sorry to think such a wish absurd and presumptuous and never to be gratified. In this world our friendships are limited to not only those who live in the same age and time but to a small portion of those who are not unknown to us and whom we know to be estimable and amiable and whom we feel might have been among our dearest friends. Our command of time and leisure to cultivate friendships poses a limit to their extent. They are bounded rather on the occupation of our thoughts. But in heaven we will have ample time for all eternity to have fellowship one with another and the Lord Jesus Christ."

And then of course there is this matter of learning. One time I heard Dr. Trumbull of the *Sunday School Times* say that when he got to heaven he would like to spend the first ten thousand years at the feet of Jesus having the Lord open to him the great treasures of the Word of God.

It is in Revelation 21:1 to 22:5 that we have the most extensive revelation of the eternal home of the redeemed, and most suitably it forms the conclusion of all the revelations of the ages recorded in our Bible. These verses, give us an unfolding and unveiling of that Holy City in which the words of our lips and the thoughts of our minds and the work of our hands and what we see and what we hear will be dominated by this basic characteristic of absolute holiness. We must not forget that what John saw was a vision. God gave it to him in such a manner that he could see this Holy City and it could be revealed in no other way.

I believe that throughout this wonderful revelation of the Holy City you have three fundamental themes here, the holiness of it, the permanence of it, and the glorious privilege of seeing the Lord and having His name stamped on our foreheads. I have heard people say: "Do you think we will know our loved ones in heaven?" My dear friend, of course we will know our loved ones in heaven. We will know millions of others too. But what makes heaven is not the fact that our loved ones will be there—that's not the first thing. The first thing will be that the Lord will be there, and we will see the Lord in all of His glory. Life divinely bestowed, then lost with sin, replaced by death, restored to us in Jesus Christ, is here set forth as the water of life and the tree of life, the total disappearance forever of the great enemy, death. Here we have a condition characterized by light—the disappearance of night. Here we have the concept of holiness which finds its roots far back in the sanctifying of the seventh day at the time of creation and which is the great objective of our redemption—we are to be holy even as He is holy. Here Glory replaces everything that may be called shameful and fragmentary, disappointing or polluting. The new will remain permanent for eternity. At last God and man shall be dwelling together—a communion never to be interrupted, and here at last we shall behold the face of Christ and shall be like Him when we shall see Him as He is.

What about the life we ought to live in the expectation of these great themes? Let me call your attention to four aspects of this, with the references, and then close with a passage from the Word of God. In the teaching of Christ, we are to be, first, like men who wait for the Lord: (Luke 12:35-38), with our loins girded about and our lamps burning. Second, we are exhorted to watchfulness (Mark 13:35). We are, third, to be faithful with the gifts that God has bestowed upon us (Matthew 25:14-30). Fourth, *Let not your heart be troubled* (John 14:1-3). Fifth, We are to be looking for the return of Christ, for the city whose builder and maker is God, as in Titus 2:13. And above all we should be filled with hope, as the Apostle Peter says: *Blessed be the God and Father of our Lord Jesus Christ, which according to his abundant mercy hath begotten us again unto a lively hope by the resurrection of Jesus Christ from the dead, to an inheritance incorruptible, and undefiled, and that fadeth not away, reserved in heaven for you, who are kept by the power of God through faith* (I Peter 1:3,4).

Now I think there is one final reference that has

nothing particularly to do with heaven but has to do with the life you and I ought to be living in the light of all we have been studying. This is from Phillips Translation, the 15th chapter of I Corinthians, concerning the resurrection. *So brothers of mine, stand firm, let nothing move you as you busy yourselves in the Lord's work. Be sure that nothing you do for him is ever lost or ever wasted.*